1991

2.95

242

SPARTA BAPTIST CHURCH
SPARTA, MICHIGAN

Please DON'T FEED THE BEARS

Please DON'T FEED THE BEARS

DELIGHTFUL STORIES FROM THE ZOO

BY GARY RICHMOND

#3767

WORD PUBLISHING
Dallas · London · Vancouver · Melbourne

SPARTA BAPTIST CHURCH
SPARTA, MICHIGAN

PLEASE DON'T FEED THE BEARS
Copyright © 1990 by Gary Richmond
All rights reserved. No portion of this book may be reproduced in any form, except brief quotations in reviews, without written permission from the publisher.

Unless otherwise indicated, Scripture quotations are from The Everyday Bible, New Century Version, copyright © 1987, 1988 by Word Publishing, Dallas, Texas 75039. Used by permission.

Photographs in this publication are by Dale Thompson and Gary Richmond.

Library of Congress Cataloging-in-Publication Data:

Richmond, Gary, 1944–
Please don't feed the bears.
1. Zoo animals—Miscellanea. 2. Animals—Miscellanea. 3. Christian life—1960– I. Title

ISBN 0–8499–0748–9
ISBN 0–8499–3193–2 (pbk.)
QL77.5.R524 1990 90–35128

0 1 2 3 9 AGF 9 8 7 6 5 4 3 2 1

Printed in the United States of America

To Carol

I want the whole world to know I love you.

Gary

A Special Thanks to:

My wife, Carol, who listened with love and did a good deal of the correction and typing of the manuscript.

My secretary, Annie Husman, whose bright, enthusiastic spirit encouraged me and who also made tons of corrections for me on the final manuscript.

My lifelong friend, Bill Welty, for reading these stories with a scholar's eye and a friend's touch. He helped make them better stories.

My best friend, Dale Thompson, who lived these adventures with me. He helped me recall them with some degree of accuracy. Dale was also my best technical adviser. He is respected in the zoo world as a world-class expert. His photography is excellent also.

My family at Word Books, for letting me serve. Kip Jordon, Ernie Owen, Joey Paul, Richard Baltzell, Laura Minchew, Nancy Guthrie, Laura Kendall, Karen Land, and my technical editor, Ed Curtis. Word is a family, and everyone is a joy to work with when doing a book.

Foreword

A View from the Zoo was a book that absolutely grabbed my mind and my heart—animal stories with a view of life. This special book was written by Gary Richmond, my friend for twenty-five years.

Gary has had many ups and downs during his twenty-seven years in the ministry. There have been moments of ecstasy and times of great disappointment. Frustrations in ministry took Gary to the Los Angeles Zoo where for seven years he served as veterinary assistant. While at the zoo, he gained great insight into animal and human behavior. These insights have given him a wonderfully rich ministry with people, particularly the past five years as the pastor to single parents at the First Evangelical Free Church of Fullerton.

During my time as the Director of Forest Home Christian Conference Center, Gary became a fixture as our real "nature" expert. I gave him the name "Father Nature" and it has stayed with him for the past sixteen years.

First came *A View from the Zoo* and now on its heels comes *Please Don't Feed the Bears*. It is graphic as well as exciting, and I know it will touch areas of your life and the life of your family. It is for the youngest child and the oldest adult.

Read and enjoy this wonderful gift from my friend!

Bob Kraning
Associate Pastor, First Evangelical Free Church, Fullerton, California
Former Director, Forest Home Christian Conference Center
Former President of Christian Camping International

Contents

Introduction

I do a lot of speaking and have a chance to share these zoo stories with thousands of people, both adults and children. They have been well received, and I hope you enjoy them. I have answered one question recently that has arisen from the hearts of honest children who simply cannot believe so many exciting things could possibly have happened to one man. They ask, "Did these stories really happen?" The answer is *yes*, they really did.

There are, of course, a handful of embellished moments. They are parts of the stories that may have been true. Let me tell you where they are for the sake of integrity.

In the story of Lobo, we never knew for sure how a timber wolf ended up at a dog pound, so I constructed a plausible beginning and end in light of the times. Everything else is true and accurate about the story.

In "The Zoo's Worst Night," the description of the security guard is a combination of two men whom the zoo keepers did not like. So this character is half real. The real men experienced enough rejection, and I did not want them to be ridiculed further.

"The Gelada" is true wherever human observation is concerned. The mountain lion, the coyote, and the rattlesnake incidents are as close as they can be to what I call possible or even likely fact . . . , or fiction. Maybe so, maybe not.

Everything else is true to my best recollection and verified by one or more people who were with me. I hope you have fun reading *Please Don't Feed the Bears*; I had fun writing it.

Your friend,

Gary Richmond

After 35 years, Toto still smiles and points to his brain on command. He was a circus chimp in his youth.

Just a Walk in the Park

The zoo security guard pulled his light green Plymouth Valiant to an abrupt halt as he approached the aquatics section. There in the lengthening shadows of early evening was a large male chimpanzee walking slowly toward the back of the California sea lion exhibit. The guard had been at the zoo long enough to recognize that this was Toto. The zoo had eight chimpanzees in the collection. Of the eight, Toto was the worst possible chimp to be three-quarters of a mile from his cage. He was a former circus chimp, and in all likelihood he had been badly abused. By human standards, Toto was crazy, psychotic, totally unpredictable. He could be gentle and friendly one moment and frenzied and violent the next.

The security guard rolled up his window and locked all the car doors. He reached for his walkie-talkie. He clicked it to the "on" position and it crackled to life. With his eyes fixed on the chimp that was now walking slowly toward his vehicle, he pressed the "send" button and whispered, "Sam, this is Joey . . . you there?"

He lifted the button and heard Sam reply, "Yeah, I'm here. What's up? Sounds like you're looking at a ghost . . . over."

"I wish I were. I'm in back of the chief keeper's shack just below the California sea lion exhibit, looking at Toto . . . over."

"Sounds like we have a problem. I'll notify the acting director and the capture team. Do your best to keep track of his whereabouts. Keep me posted. And Joey, be real careful. From what I've heard, Toto is bad news."

Joey kept track of Toto, and for whatever reason, Toto stayed near the chief's shack. He was, for all intents and purposes, lost. His zoo cage had been his territory for two years, and without help he would not be able to find his way back to it. Not knowing where he was, Toto was left with the problem of having nowhere to run. In his tangled mind he imagined he could be in enemy-occupied territory and was on the verge of emotional frenzy. He probably stayed in the area to be near the security guard who was keeping an eye on him.

Most of the capture team arrived at the same time and wisely stayed in their cars, waiting for Dr. Gale, the assistant director. Dr. Gale was an excellent animal-capture man worth waiting for, and the truth was that he would not have tolerated it any other way.

Toto was preoccupied with the sounds and smells of the immediate area and was satisfied that his company was staying in their cars. When Dr. Gale arrived, it was very dark and only the horizon gave a hint that the sun had just set for the night. The zoo's dark green shrubbery nearly absorbed Toto's silhouette, and only his occasional movement betrayed his whereabouts. Dr. Gale directed the security guard to watch Toto, then motioned for the capture team to follow him out of the area. Once out of

Toto's sight, they got out of their cars and listened to Dr. Gale's plan.

"We can't dart Toto with the capture gun; it is too dark to know if we hit him. He might fall into a pool, or worst of all, we may miss and scare him so that he leaves the zoo. Then he'd need to be shot before he hurt someone in the local neighborhood. If any of you have change, give it to me." They looked at each other, wondering what Dr. Gale had up his sleeve. But they knew him well enough not to question him. The change added up to a little less than two dollars. Dr. Gale sighed as he held it in his hand. He gave Bob Spellings fifty cents of it and told him to run and get a Coke from the nearest vending machine. He told the other men to drive up to the zoo's health center, open all the doors, and wait there for him and Toto. He told them he was going to attempt to walk Toto back to his cage; but he felt the fewer animal-care staff that Toto saw, the less chance there would be of Toto's flipping out and becoming violent.

Bob Spelling returned with the Coke and handed it to Dr. Gale who took a sip, and smiled a "wish-me-luck" smile. He waited for the men to clear the area, then walked slowly toward Toto. When he was nearing the escaped chimp he could see that Toto was a bit apprehensive, and even in the dark he could see that Toto was beginning to stand; his hair was on end, and he looked as if he were about to charge.

Dr. Gale spoke softly, "You want something to drink, Toto?" Toto settled down and walked slowly forward and looked briefly at the cup and then into Dr. Gale's eyes. He reached for the man's hand and pulled it and the cup to his mouth and moaned contentedly. He poured most of the cup into his mouth. Dr. Gale was wishing the zoo served larger Cokes, because his plan was to lure him from vending machine to vending machine until they reached Toto's cage. But if Toto were going to finish everything so quickly, he might not follow to the next reward. Even worse, he might want more, and there would be no more to give him. It never took much to disturb Toto, and that was the last thing Dr. Gale wanted to happen alone in the dark in the middle of the zoo. He was already questioning the wisdom of his own plan and looked around to see if any of the men were still nearby to suggest Plan B. But he was alone. He wasn't really alone; there was a psychotic former circus chimp standing at his side drinking the last drop of Coke out of a cup that seemed smaller than ever.

Dr. Gale saw the chief keeper's building and concluded that he might buy some time if he could lock Toto in the building. So he offered Toto his hand, and Toto took it—something he would have done as a young chimp but may not do for long as an old chimp who was six times as strong as the man who was leading him. Dr. Gale removed his keys from his pocket and unlocked the chief keeper's office. He walked into the dark office, hoping Toto would follow. He did. It was darker inside than out and Dr. Gale waited until he was sure Toto was fully inside.

Then Dr. Gale made a quick move and slipped out the door as quickly as he could. He slammed the door and locked it. His heart was pounding and beads of perspiration were forming on his forehead. He wiped it with his handkerchief and walked on his tiptoes to see if Toto was calmly inside. He shaded his eyes from the glare of the street light that created reflections on the window and stared into the darkness of the office. He strained his eyes to see Toto, but could not locate the chimp. He felt a hand on his shoulder and slowly turned to find himself face to face with a disturbed Toto. In a mimicking fashion, Toto was also shielding his eyes from the reflection as he, too, stared into the darkness, trying to discover what had frightened the doctor out of the office.

"Let's go home, Toto," said the doctor, resigned to the first plan. Toto followed him to the next vending machine where he purchased a small box of Good and Plenty candies. Toto enjoyed them immensely, but he would stop, sit down, and suck on them, so progress was somewhat impeded. Dr. Gale was limited to one more purchase, and he was not even half way to the health center. The wizened vet noticed a drinking fountain and turned the handle to show Toto that he could get a drink. Toto drank copious drafts of water and was captured by the novelty of the drinking device.

A lion roared from its night quarters. Toto stood straight up and rocked back and forth as if he were going to begin an aggressive display. He ran toward the lion and screamed one loud scream as a warning to his unseen enemy. Then he looked back at Dr. Gale as if to say, "Well, I guess that takes care of that." Dr. Gale praised him in a soft voice and rewarded him with a Good and Plenty.

The Good and Plenty ran out, so he made one last purchase. A Payday candy bar slid out of the vending machine. Toto watched with interest as its wrapper was peeled away and a small piece was handed to him. Dr. Gale walked faster now, knowing he was on borrowed time. Toto grunted a "wait for me" sound and ran on all fours to catch up. The Payday was clearly a favorite choice. The chimp tugged at his benefactor's pant leg for another piece. Progress was now at a sufficient pace, and it looked as though they might make it to the health center after all.

As they rounded the corner at the mountain zebra exhibit, a terror-filled event took place. Ed Alonzo, the principal keeper, was waiting fifty yards away under a street light, monitoring the doctor's journey. If Dr. Gale got in trouble, Ed wanted to be there to help. But now Ed was in trouble. When Toto saw Ed under the street light, he stood up and hooted. He bolted away from Dr. Gale and ran at full speed toward the frozen principal keeper. Toto had injured others, and Ed fully expected to be bitten and beaten within an inch of his life, so he braced himself for the attack.

Toto looked menacing as he charged closer and closer. Ed swallowed and prepared himself for the awesome impact he was about to experience. At the last possible second, Toto pulled up short and stood up in front of Ed to greet him. Ed had been his keeper a few years before, and Toto was merely saying hello with a great deal of enthusiasm. Seeing a person that Toto remembered fondly had thoroughly piqued his interest. He had grown tired of the night's adventure, and Ed probably represented care and security. Toto reached for Ed's hand, which was shaking noticeably from the massive dose of adrenalin which had just been released into his system. The baton had been handed to Ed, so the last one hundred yards were his to accomplish.

He and Toto walked up a narrow overgrown path, and when they reached the top, they could see the health center in full view. Toto released Ed's hand and again ran full speed until he had entered the health center's surgery door. He walked down the well-lighted hallway into the cage room and stood peering through the open door of his cage as if he were trying to make up his mind, "Shall I go in, or shall I stay out?" It was at this point that Bill Dickman, a brave and foolish keeper, ran full swing into Toto, bumping him into his cage and slamming the door behind him. Toto hooted his displeasure, but he decided to be forgiving because he was so glad to be home.

This story reminds me that Jesus was willing to leave the safety of heaven to help me find my way back to Him. He cared about you and me so much that no risk was too great to ensure that we could come home. There was one difference in His story, however. He died to make it possible. During our lives two things will always be true: (1) We will need to help others find the way to Jesus. (2) We will need to help Christians who have lost their way to find their way home. We *are* our brother's keeper.

Orangutans are my favorite animals. Everything they do is fun to watch.

This baby Gorilla strikes a thoughtful pose. Much of what they do is hauntingly human.

The Red Fox is a study in soft beauty and as shrewd as rumored.

Few animals can relax like Hippos. Their secret — a clear conscience.

When this Bengal Tiger looked at the curator and the two keepers in his cage, they thought their life was over.

The Polar Bear can weigh up to 1,600 pounds and has the pulling power of 30 men.

This mother Kangaroo has a Joey (a baby) that even as a teenager climbs into the pouch.

Please Don't Feed the Bears

It was late in the afternoon when we pulled up to the office of Moore's Redwoods. We had rented a cabin for a week and needed only to pick up our key so that our vacation could really begin. My wife Carol and I entered the office, glad to be out of the car and anxious to explore our cabin. We were greeted by the manager, a woman in her early sixties. She wore horn-rimmed glasses and welcomed us with a raspy voice, a product of 40-plus years of smoking. She acquainted us with the campground's rules and pointed out the numerous opportunities for recreation in the area. Much was available because Moore's Redwoods was a group of privately owned cabins located in the midst of the most majestic national park in the world, Yosemite.

A week would never be enough time to see Yosemite's beauty, but we were going to try. As we were leaving the office, the manager added, "Oh, by the way, don't feed the bears. We've got a big sow and her cub coming through every night, and she's a mean one; big one, too. She's threatened some folks and could be dangerous."

I nodded. I didn't know what Carol was thinking, but I was wondering where one might purchase bear food. I wanted to see this mean old she-bear and her cub and make sure our vacation had a smidge of adventure to flavor the relaxation.

I also wanted to call the Guinness Book of World Records people to find out if our six-year-old daughter Marci had asked "Are we there yet?" more times in a six-hour period than any child before her. I opted for unloading our Buick Estate station wagon instead. During the unloading process, I discovered why they had called it the Estate—you could haul everything you owned inside and on top of it. It felt more like a move than a trip. Oh, the sweet relief of carrying the last piece of luggage into the cabin. I flopped down on the couch to rest, closed my eyes, and stretched out. I kicked off my shoes, and wiggled into a comfortable position. I took a deep breath, letting the air out slowly as I always do just before I nap. It was then that the Stealth-bomber prototype dropped her thirty-pound payload to my midsection from the back of the couch and asked if I wanted to play. I have never abused my children, but at that moment, as I was falling asleep thinking about mean bears, whatever I might have done would have been in self-defense. However, I restrained myself and only went for my daughter's throat for a second.

There is one sentence whose meaning I could never teach to my children: "Daddy's tired." They always stared blankly, asking again and again if I wanted to play. I was twenty-seven at the time and still hadn't answered the question "Why did we have children?"

Carol fixed a wonderful dinner that evening, and we ate it on the deck in front of the cabin. The sun silhouetted a thousand pine trees as it set in the west. The fragrance of pine burning in a dozen fireplaces mixed with the clean mountain air and revived us. As a family of deer walked through camp, we joined other families in feeding them bread and black oak leaves. This was a preview of heaven's coming attractions, and I thought as I looked at my family and smelled the air, "It doesn't get any better than this."

We were not able to eat all that Carol had prepared, and I was glad. We had bear bait. I gathered the bits of corn and salad and placed chicken bones with meat over the top of it all. I laid it carefully on a paper plate near the bottom of the metal trash can. Then I placed the lid on the trash can and put a fifty-pound rock on the lid. Around the rock I sprinkled bits of chicken. If this didn't attract the she-bear, nothing would. We weren't sure when she would come through the campground, but I knew I would hear her if she did. As an afterthought, I stacked seven aluminum cans in a pyramid on top of the trash can. When the she-bear moved that lid, we would know it.

Dishes were cleaned and put away. Then we played Scrabble. Carol won. We had brought good books, and after putting the girls to bed, we began to read them.

At 9:30 P.M. I heard the cans fall. The she-bear was just outside our kitchen window. We turned out the lights in the cabin, and Carol and I walked to the kitchen sink. We pulled the curtains apart slowly and peeked through. We were shocked to find that she was only four feet away. She was standing, and she was massive. The street lights provided a little illumination so we saw her fairly well. The night was very foggy and, because it was mid-June, still very cold. Steam was billowing from her mouth and nostrils in the 60-degree air. She looked dark and sinister. The cans had apparently frightened her cubs, and she was clearly postured to protect them. We finally saw them. The cubs were near the trash can trying to pull it over. They could not because it was held fast by a steel frame.

The she-bear grabbed the 50-pound rock and pushed it several feet from the garbage can. She deftly pulled off the lid and tried to reach the chicken near the bottom of the can. Failing, she just stuck the top third of her body in the can and stood up again with chicken, corn, and a paper plate in her mouth. She had to weigh 500 pounds and was easily the largest black bear I had ever seen.

She finished the food from the garbage can and moaned at her cubs. They were quick to snap to attention and follow her into the foggy night.

It had been a thrill being that close to such an obviously dangerous animal. But that thrill was to pale in comparison with a coming thrill.

The next day we drove into Yosemite Valley, and all of us were impressed with its majesty. The snow pack in the upper meadows was more than adequate to create a massive run-off. All the falls were thundering. Spray was blowing everywhere. No matter where you look in Yosemite, the effect is awe. There just isn't a greater example of God's handiwork anywhere on the earth.

We visited the ranger station where there was a display showing the destructive power of bears. There were many examples of bent metal and broken doors, all of which provided evidence to help you to conclude, "DON'T FEED THE BEARS."

The display didn't tell any specific stories but hinted that many visitors to the park had suffered injuries from bears. The display was intended to convince you that letting bears be bears and not associating with them was clearly the best course to take if you wanted to go home in one piece.

For some the display was all that would be needed to help them behave responsibly. For a few of us it was more fuel for the fire. It made bears seem that much more exciting to play with.

Late that afternoon we were joined at our cabin by the Crosleys, who were close friends from San Jose. They brought their handsome toddler, Greg, and planned to spend the next three days with us and our two daughters,

Marci and Wendi. Fine times are always best enjoyed with good friends. Knowing Rich was a kindred spirit, I could hardly wait to share the bear adventure with him. Rich was a jet pilot and loved adventure as much as I did.

I was right. Rich was wild about the idea of baiting the she-bear and getting a good look at her. We barbequed again, and the leftovers were perfect bear bait.

This time it was steak, beans, and bits and pieces of dessert and salad. Rich and I lovingly collected the garbage and again broke the rules by baiting the garbage can. Our wives protested, saying that they made these rules for good reasons and we ought to follow them. Well, what could you expect? They had both willingly journeyed through adolescence into adulthood. Rich and I, on the other hand, were firmly attached to childhood with no intention of letting go.

I tried to explain to our wives that, being a junior animal authority, I knew what I was doing. "There are only two rules that will guarantee our safety," I proclaimed. "Number one, don't get between the sow and her cubs. Number two, don't get very close to the female."

Well, after a little debate, Rich and I wore them down.

We played Rook, a sort of a poor man's Bridge, guys against the girls, for two hours. Then we heard the sound of crashing aluminum cans. The she-bear was back.

We turned out all the lights and gathered around the kitchen sink to see her. We carefully separated the curtains, and there she was. She had already cast aside the large rock, and we watched her snap the lid off the can. She didn't bother about reaching for the food; she just bent over and began devouring the morsels left for her. We could hear the steak bones cracking. She chewed them like potato chips. It was an eerie sound. She stood and sniffed at the air. Again billows of steam issued forth in clouds from her nostrils and mouth. Our hearts all stopped when she turned and looked directly through the window at us. She was definitely a scary looking bear. We could see her brown-stained teeth as she licked the grease from her lips and muzzle.

She looked away, and we breathed again. She called her cubs, and they followed her toward the front of the cabin.

"Rich, let's see where she goes from here," I said. He nodded and, much to the frustration of our wives, we stepped out on the front porch.

We saw her in the glow of the street light as she lumbered slowly west. Her incredible size was accented by the cub walking next to her. The fog-draped landscape they entered would have made an ideal scene for a horror movie.

Now something was wrong with this picture of the she-bear and the lone cub, but we didn't realize immediately what it was. Inside the cabin, Carol was looking out the kitchen window and noticed another cub. It had doubled back to look for more scraps of food. Carol remembered what I had said about getting between a mother and her cubs and knew Rich and I were in trouble. She ran to the front door of the cabin to warn us and found the door wedged tight. Assuming it was locked, she turned the door handle and inadvertently locked it.

Outside, Rich and I had brazenly walked down the steps to get a better look at the mother bear when I heard the second of her cubs cry out behind us. I don't know what it said, but my guess is that it saw us and called out for help. This mother was a good mother and would tolerate no remote possibility that harm would befall her cubs. She was about fifty yards away when she began to charge. She roared, and it was clear we were in trouble.

I was in front of Rich and turned to run to the cabin. Rich, not yet aware of the second cub, turned to see why the mother roared. I ran right into him, knocking him flat. As I picked him up, I shouted, "RUN!" Rich's military training and view of the she-bear encouraged him to respond quickly. We were both covering a lot of territory at a cartoon pace, clouds of dust, no doubt, billowing behind us. We made the stairs that led to the cabin deck and were up all six of them in two strides. I could hear the bear's breathing and growling just behind. If she had caught us (I don't even care to think about it), I am sure it would have made headlines.

TWO PRE-ADULTS CAUGHT FEEDING BEAR
BEAR PLEADS JUSTIFIABLE HOMICIDE

I reached the door first, turned the handle, and pushed with all my might. My mistaken impression was that we had been locked out. The reality was that Carol was trying to get the door open from the other side. She was finally able to move it into the unlocked position, and we scrambled inside, slamming the door behind us. I threw myself against the door and waited for 500 pounds of anger to attempt to break it down.

It was silent except for the heavy breathing of four terrified adults.

Several seconds passed, and there were no bear sounds of any kind. None on the porch and none outside. Our wives, who by this time had run into the bedroom to hide, came out and cautiously peeked through the window. They saw no evidence of bears anywhere. The bears were mercifully gone. I sank into a chair and wiped the perspiration off my forehead. We all began to laugh. It was nervous laughter at first but turned to the boy-was-that-a-stupid-thing-to-do kind.

There is no teacher like experience. I don't even have to see a sign or be told "Please don't feed the bears" anymore. Close calls don't get any closer than that without becoming a needless tragedy. The memory is funny because I can laugh at my humanity and because I am alive to tell the story.

Feeding the bears had an obvious consequence: the possibility of bodily harm. And there are other "please don'ts" that do, also. Please don't drink and drive is one of them. Smoking may be hazardous to your health is another. We are surrounded by warnings. If we ignore them, there will certainly be consequences.

God's most important list of don'ts is found in the Old Testament book of Exodus, chapter 20. They are considerably less optional than "Please don't feed the bears." Ignoring or violating them is sure to produce consequences. Have you reviewed them lately? Have you ever pondered the consequences?

Commandment 1. "You must not have any other gods except me" (Exod. 20:3).

Consequence of Disobedience: Should you decide not to let God be God, then you will face life without His help and eternity without His presence. John the Baptist said that "he who believes in the Son has eternal life. But he who does not obey the Son will never have that life. God's anger stays with him" (John 3:36).

Commandment 2. "You must not make for yourselves any idols. Don't make something that looks like anything in the sky above or on the earth below or in the water below the land. You must not worship or serve any idol" (Exod. 20:4–5).

Consequence of Disobedience: "This is because I, the Lord your God, am a jealous God. A person may sin against me and hate me. I will punish his children, even his grandchildren and great-grandchildren" (Exod. 20:5). This is an awesome warning involving the welfare of our children.

Commandment 3. "You must not use the name of the Lord your God thoughtlessly" (Exod. 20:7a).

Consequence of Disobedience: "The Lord will punish anyone who is guilty and misuses his name" (Exod 20:7b). God does not tell us the consequence but assures us there will be one.

Commandment 4. "Remember to keep the Sabbath as a holy day. You may work and get everything done during six days each week. But the seventh day is a day of rest to honor the Lord your God. On that day no one may do any work: not you, your son or daughter, or your men or women slaves. Neither your animals nor the foreigners living in your cities may work. The reason is that in six days the Lord made everything. He made the sky, earth, sea and everything in them. And on the seventh day, he rested. So the Lord blessed the Sabbath day and made it holy" (Exod. 20:8–11).

Consequence of Disobedience: The consequences are threefold: physical and spiritual exhaustion and the missing of an opportunity to fulfill the purpose for which we were made, to glorify God through obedience and worship. Every Sabbath missed cannot be made up. It's just missed. It's a zero in the grade book. You will be restless.

Commandment 5. "Honor your father and your mother. Then you will live a long time in the land. The Lord your God is going to give you this land" (Exod. 20:12).

Consequence of Disobedience: The term "live a long time" means have a full, satisfying life. If you dishonor your parents, you will fill your life with chaos. You will not find peace, but you will find yourself running on empty without the ability to be satisfied. I have yet to know a happy person at odds with his parents.

Commandment 6. "You must not murder anyone" (Exod. 20:13).

Consequence of Disobedience: You forfeit your right to life. "Whoever kills a human being will be killed by a human being. This is because God made humans in his own image" (Gen. 9:6).

Commandment 7. "You must not be guilty of adultery" (Exod. 20:14).

Consequence of Disobedience: These consequences are especially severe. "A man who takes part in adultery doesn't have any sense. He will destroy himself. He will be beaten up and disgraced. And his shame will never go away" (Prov. 6:32–33).

Commandment 8. "You must not steal" (Exod. 20:15).

Consequence of Disobedience: The thief will be thought of as useless (Eph. 4:28). The thief must give back what he took plus one fifth and make an offering to the Lord (Lev. 6:4–6).

Commandment 9. "You must not tell lies about your neighbor in court" (Exod. 20:16).

Consequence of Disobedience: Lying is definitely considered a serious sin with harsh consequences. "The mouths of liars will be shut," writes David in Psalm 63:11. "It is better to be poor than to be a liar" (Prov. 19:22). Lying makes you like Satan (John 8:44). "[The Lord] destroy[s] liars. The Lord hates those who kill and trick others" (Ps. 5:6). The Lord hates liars, considers them like the evil one, and he will shut them up. I'd say these are consequences, serious consequences.

Commandment 10. "You must not want to take your neighbor's house. You must not want his wife or his men or women slaves. You must not want his ox or his donkey. You must not want to take anything that belongs to your neighbor" (Exod. 20:17).

Consequence of Disobedience: Although there is no specific Scripture that spells out the consequences of coveting, there are stories that illustrate its effect. To covet is to have an inordinate desire to possess something belonging to someone else. One consequence of coveting is a pervasive feeling of dissatisfaction. In that way you punish yourself.

When David saw Bathsheba on the rooftop bathing, he wanted her for himself. But she was married to one of his most faithful soldiers. That was coveting. When he gave in to coveting, it ruined the rest of his life. He was never really happy again.

Closing thought: Just as there are severe consequences for breaking God's standards of behavior, there are even greater rewards for keeping them. "But I will be very kind to thousands who love me and obey my commands" (Exod. 20:6).

A Cobra's Loose

The keepers at the reptile house usually begin their day at 8:30 A.M., just like most of the keepers at the zoo. When I worked there, some keepers started earlier than that, but not many. Those men with responsibilities in the larger enclosures could not finish their tasks by 10:00 if they started at 8:30, so they tended to start earlier.

After the reptile keepers signed in on the daily log, the senior keeper walked around the display area, looking carefully at each aquarium to see how the reptiles were doing. He did this to ensure that the zoo was not exhibiting any dead animals. Exhibiting dead animals would cut down on the food bill, but it tended to disturb the children who visited the zoo. Our director would have had a fit if he heard that the public had discovered a dead animal before the animal services staff found it.

The morning rounds could take anywhere from thirty

to forty minutes if you were thorough. The zoo had a large collection of snakes, lizards, frogs, toads, and turtles to be checked.

One Tuesday morning, Bill Welty, the senior keeper, began his rounds. Bill was the thorough type and stared intently into each cage, looking briefly at each animal until he was sure that it was breathing.

It was a beautiful spring morning, and Bill found himself in no particular hurry to complete his task. He had finished two-thirds of his task when he saw something that froze the marrow in his bones. There was broken glass on the pavement up ahead and a log sticking two feet outside the cage. He knew exactly which cage had been breached. He ran forward but slowed and approached the display carefully, taking one cautious step after another.

The closer he got the more obvious it became that a large portion of glass had been broken, leaving a massive escape door for the reptile.

"Oh, no!" he said out loud as he read the label above the cage: "Spitting Cobra." He stared into the cage hoping that the snake had decided to stay, but it hadn't. The cage was empty. A log that had been bolted to the cage wall had come loose and fallen forward, breaking the glass outward.

Bill knew time was of the essence, but it was still hard to run to the emergency phone and call the assistant director. He was a man who had almost no tolerance for bad news and an obsession with fixing blame. Bill began to walk quickly and then, grasping fully the gravity of the problem, he began to run for the phone.

Bill dialed Dr. Creighton's extension. His heart began to pound, partly because of the realization that a cobra was loose in the zoo one hour before it was due to open, but mostly because of his reluctance to be the messenger of bad news to Dr. Creighton.

"Yes," snapped Dr. Creighton.

"Bill Welty, sir. We have an emergency. A log came

loose from the wall and broke the front of the Spitting Cobra's cage. He's out in the zoo."

Dr. Creighton was a man of few words and simply said, "You and your men start looking for it." Then he hung up.

Bill stared at the phone, placed it on the receiver, and gathered his men.

"A Spitting Cobra's loose, guys. Grab some nets and nooses, and let's go find it."

Mickey Knight, Bill's most outspoken keeper, said, "If we don't find that thing, they can't open the zoo, can they?"

"Mickey, it's comforting to know that you have a firm grasp on the obvious. We're going to find it or one of us, maybe more, will be zoo visitors instead of zoo employees. Grasp that!"

Back at Dr. Creighton's office, the assistant director had leapt from his desk and stood before his secretary barking out orders: "A cobra is loose in the zoo. Call security and have them keep the front gates closed to the public until I tell them different. Call the chief keeper and have him send every keeper at the zoo to the reptile house within ten minutes. That's where I'll be. Tell everyone that this is hush-hush. I don't want this to make the news with any 'film at eleven'!

When Dr. Creighton arrived at the reptile house, the three keepers and their senior were walking around the area, attempting to locate the deadly serpent. They were carrying bird nets and poles with nooses on one end.

Dr. Creighton made a point of checking the broken glass, and, unable to trust anyone, he also checked the cage to make sure that the cobra was actually gone. Satisfied, he joined the keepers in the search.

He found a long stick and did what no one up to that point had done. He began poking around in the eight-inch deep ivy. He stepped into it and began to walk around in it slowly, his ankles and shins completely hidden in the shiny green foliage.

Dr. Creighton was in many ways a tyrant, but a tyrant with a backbone. He was, as I remember, a man without fear. I worked for him for six years and in all sorts of harrowing adventures. I never saw fear on his face even once. I never even saw a surprised look on his face.

Keepers from other sections began arriving, but not all forty-seven. In fact, over the next hour only fifteen showed to help find the cobra. Seven were supervisors who were more afraid of Dr. Creighton than the snake. The children's zoo attendants, all ladies, were not invited to the safari, so it meant that twenty-three men were hiding. Twenty-three men decided that they wanted nothing to do with a spitting cobra that was bent on freedom. Some keepers actually hid in the shrubbery rather than be in a position to be rounded up. The truth is, most keepers who loved animals in general were afraid of snakes specifically. They would have quit before taking a chance with that cobra.

Mickey Knight joined Dr. Creighton in the ivy, convinced that that was where the snake would have chosen to hide. Knowing Mickey, I would say that he was tromping around in the ivy, not because of an overabundance of courage, but because of a serious deficiency of common sense.

Neither of the men knew for sure where the snake was, but logic and intuition pointed them to that location. There was really no telling where it might have crawled. It had had plenty of time to crawl anywhere.

The fact is both men were right. The snake was with them in the ivy. Cobras see very well, and this one was following every move of both men. It was five and a half feet long and a faded brownish black. Its color was blending with the dead vines and leaves beneath the canopy of green. The men had actually looked directly at the snake several times, but its color blended in well and its absolute stillness made it impossible to see.

For a moment everyone froze when they heard Jim Boice scream and jump back from the shrubbery. Several men joined Jim to see what was up. He was hyperventilating and holding his heart. "I think I saw it behind that bush," he said. Everyone stepped back and Dr. Creighton came through, pushing men out of his way. He fearlessly leaned over the bush and stared into the shade behind it.

All of a sudden he reached down and grabbed at something. He pulled out a length of black rubber tubing and tossed it at the feet of a group of disturbed keepers. As they scattered he said, "The crisis isn't over. Let's keep looking." He returned to the ivy along with Mickey Knight.

Mickey, entertained by what Dr. Creighton had done, was acting a little silly in the ivy. He was leaping up and down and calling out "Come out, come out, wherever you are." When he stepped on the cobra's tail, it did just that. Mickey didn't see it, but others did and sucked in their breath waiting for it to strike him.

The cobra was trembling with excitement and rage. Its eyes were following Mickey's every movement as he jumped around next to the snake. The cobra had raised its head out of the ivy, and about two feet of it was clearly visible.

Finally Mickey saw it and leapt backward to gain a little distance. As he did, he made a funny sound, something between an "oooof!" and an "ahhhh!" His eyes were large and riveted on the snake. He quickly regained his composure and judged himself to be out of spitting distance from the angry reptile. The snake could spray venom about six feet with total accuracy. If Mickey was not careful, he would be blinded from the venom.

Mickey extended his pole toward the snake, slipped the noose over its head, and pulled it tight. The snake writhed and hissed, but it was firm in grasp of the noose at 9:56 A.M.

Dr. Creighton commended Mickey and told him to carry the snake into the reptile house as quickly as possible. There was no need to draw this out. Dr. Creighton called security from the reptile house office.

"The cobra's been secured. You can let the patrons in the zoo."

The head of security said, "I'm glad you got him because if you hadn't I wasn't going to come into the zoo myself."

There are lots of escapes that the public never hears about. This was just one of them. It had a grand conclusion and a happy ending because of a handful of men who refused to be afraid. They knew that nothing could be done until the snake was brought into the light. If it remained hidden, the zoo would have been a dangerous place for years to come. This was not the only time a hidden snake was to complicate my life. A boa constrictor did it the next time.

It was the middle of September, and, boy, was it hot. For two consecutive weeks the temperatures had been resting in the high nineties every afternoon. I was booked to speak in Barstow at a Campus Life Saturday night rally, and I had to be there at 6:00 P.M. Barstow is in the Mojave Desert, and they had been seeing temperatures soar to 110 degrees Fahrenheit.

My car didn't have air conditioning, and I was supposed to take a large South American redtail boa constrictor named Samson with me. Hundreds would disappointed if he did not show, but the car would reach temperatures beyond Samson's level of tolerance. The drive might kill him. I shared my dilemma with my wife, Carol, and she reminded me that her mother had offered the use of their air-conditioned Dodge Dart if we needed it.

I picked up the car, loaded slide projectors and slides in the trunk, and put Samson on the front seat next to me. I carried Samson in a pillowcase that always attracted attention. It had Juvenile Hall written across the top of it because that's where it had come from. Carol had gotten it from her sister Darla, who had helped at Juvenile Hall while she was in nursing school. The pillowcase was well worn by a lot of ill-behaved teenaged heads. I was aware that it would soon be time to get a new one but not aware enough as it turned out.

I allowed two and one-half hours to get there. Because of the efficiency of the air conditioning, Samson and I arrived rested and ready to go. As soon as I opened the car door, the heat hit us like a blast furnace. I was sure that Samson would never have made the trip alive without the air conditioning.

I was greeted by wonderfully friendly people who were glad to help me unload everything but Samson. They decided I could accomplish that without their help. But I was used to that response. People would feel differently after the program when they saw young children petting and holding the docile predator without incident.

They opened their program with music, singing, and announcements. In no time they were introducing me. "Ladies and gentlemen, all the way from the Los Angeles Zoo with a fascinating program illustrated with beautiful slides is our guest speaker, Gary Richmond. Let's give him a warm Barstow welcome." I hoped it wouldn't be too warm because the air conditioning where we met was inadequate for the heat wave they were experiencing. Though the crowd seemed acclimated to the eighty-seven-degree gymnasium, Samson and I were not. I was drenched in perspiration, and Samson was trying his best to get out of the pillowcase so he could find a cooler place to rest.

I was glad when the lights were turned out so that the enormous sweat rings that had appeared on my shirt would no longer be visible. My talk went fine, and they were an enchanting and responsive audience. When the lights were again turned on, I leaned to the microphone and said, "If you will relax for one minute, I will bring out a friend of mine that many of you have been waiting to meet." I stepped down off the stage to get Samson, but my heart sank as I felt the empty pillowcase. Samson was somewhere in a crowd of three hundred people, and I didn't know where.

I stepped back to the microphone and said, "Ladies and gentleman, I'm going to ask you to trust me completely for your good, my good, and Samson the boa constrictor's good. You need to know that he is very tame. He has never bitten anyone ever. You have nothing to fear when I say he has escaped." There was a bit of murmuring. "Do not leave your seats, but please look under them. If you see him, raise your hand, and I will come and pick him up." It was funny to see everybody bend over slowly to see if Samson had chosen them. Nobody raised a hand, and some began to think they were being put on.

"One second," I asked. I jumped off the stage and walked around the crowd to see if Samson was against the wall. As soon as I saw a stack of gymnastic mats, I knew where I would find him. I pulled them away from the wall, and there he was. As I picked up the snake, the crowd clapped and cheered. There was suddenly a circus atmosphere, and everyone enjoyed an all's-well-that-ends-well moment. Scores of people held and touched the snake. He turned out to be the highlight of the evening.

When I picked up the pillowcase, I discovered the large hole through which he had escaped. He must have flexed and torn the case in the heat of the evening. Before putting him in again, I tied a knot in the end of the pillowcase. We loaded the car and I was off for home. It was 9:30, and I expected to be home about midnight. I turned on the radio, and as I sat back to relax, I reached over and patted Samson. I patted him for two reasons. First, I appreciated the addition he had been to the program and told him so, although, being a snake, he had no ears and could not hear me. Second, I patted him to make sure that he was still in the pillowcase. If he had escaped once, he could do it again. I could feel his muscular body tense to my touch then relax.

There is nothing more wonderful than a California desert night. The temperature was now in the low eighties, and I was intoxicated by the fragrance of the sand, sagebrush, and yuccas that were silhouetted against the black-velvet, star-studded sky. The windows were down, and there was virtually no traffic. Even at seventy miles per hour (the speed limit then), the ride seemed relaxed and the progress seemed minimal. But that was okay because I was enraptured by the number of stars spread out before me. They looked three dimensional. The lights of the city block out all but the larger stars, so it was refreshing to enjoy God's spectacular handiwork at its best.

I tuned into a powerful radio station and enjoyed Peter, Paul, and Mary, Diana Ross, The Beatles, and a witty disc jockey as I sped homeward. As I reached over to pat Samson again, my heart skipped a beat. The pillowcase was empty.

I pulled the car over to the side of the road and skidded to a stop. I turned on the overhead light and began looking under the front seats and the dash board without success. I began to feel into places that I could not see, desperate to find the escape-artist snake. I noticed that the air-conditioning vents were very large and suspected that Samson had crawled into one of them. I reached into them as far as I could. Samson was tame, but sometimes when tame snakes are again free they will make an exception to their normal behavior and bite to stay free.

I wondered where the air conditioning vent led. I wondered if a snake could crawl through and fall onto the road. He certainly did not seem to be in the car. I put my ear to the vent and held my breath to see if I could hear any movement. I could not. Samson was either gone or at rest.

Now this situation was not good for two reasons. One, Samson was not my snake, and, two, this was not my car. I had always enjoyed a terrific relationship with my mother-in-law, but I felt that returning the car to her, not knowing for sure whether a large boa constrictor was a silent passenger, who might turn up again in freeway traffic, could put a bit of a strain on that relationship. Who was I kidding? She'd never speak to me again. I was sick.

I started the car and headed for home. How was I

going to tell my best friend, Dale, that I had lost his snake—that Samson may have been the victim of the next eighteen-wheeler to come down the highway? Samson a frisbee. What a horrible thought!

But was it more horrible than the thought of Samson still in the car, carefully hidden in hundred-degree weather? The car could only be driven at night until we knew for sure where he was. If a snake Samson's size were to die undiscovered, he would begin to smell in a day and no one would ever be able to drive the car again. Nothing dies as convincingly as a snake. No odor approximates a dead snake. Look in the dictionary under stench, and you'll see a picture of a dead snake.

How was I going to tell Carol that Samson was lost in her mother's new car? I prayed for wisdom, the rapture, a silver tongue. Help!

When I got home, it was a little before midnight. Carol was still up, and she was very understanding. We got a flashlight and looked again to find Samson. When we didn't find him, I suggested that I ought to find an all-night garage so that I might at least ask a mechanic whether a snake could crawl through the vents and fall on the road. If Samson could still be in the car, it must be parked in a very shady place so that the car would not overheat and kill him. We would need to buy time to find him.

I pulled into a gas station in Highland Park, a suburb of Los Angeles, and got out of my car. The all-night mechanic on duty greeted me and asked how he could help me. I wasn't sure how to begin. No matter how I framed my question, I was going to come off as some kind of nutball.

"I have a hypothetical question," I said hesitantly.

"Hypothetical?" he queried. I wondered if maybe he didn't know what hypothetical meant because most of his customers just had questions, straightforward, normal, everyday questions. Shoot, I wished I had one.

I opened the passenger door and pointed to the air conditioning vent, which was well illuminated, and asked,

"If something about ten inches around, say as big around as a large navel orange, crawled in this hole, would it be able to crawl all the way out of the car and drop onto the highway?" As I was speaking I knew I sounded a little irrational. I could see it in his eyes. They had narrowed, and he had stepped back from the car.

"Jus' what's da sumpin' what's crawled in da vent?" he asked with a good deal of skepticism.

I didn't want to admit that a boa constrictor was loose in the car, so I said, "Something about the size of a really big rat." Then I realized that anyone who didn't like snakes wouldn't likely be fond of big rats either. The whites of his eyes showed me that.

"They's a ten-inch-around rat in yo air vent?"

"Well, no," I admitted. "Something the size of a rat, a real big rat is in there unless he was able to crawl through. If he could crawl through, then he's history. He's part of the pavement in the Mojave Desert."

He took another step back. "Les 'stablish sumpin'. Dis conversation is comin' to a quick halt les you tells me what in there. Sumpin' like a real big rat don't sound like to me is a rat. What is in there?"

I was caught. "Well, I know this sounds kind of silly, but I work at the Los Angeles Zoo and I speak a lot to schools and organizations and church groups and things like that and I sometimes take my best friend's boa constrictor with . . ." That's when I lost him. He jumped away from the car.

"You means to tell me you almos' had me pokin' aroun' fo a big snake? You got dus' fo brains or sumpin'? I'm tellin' ya. Shoot, man, I can't believe it. Ya see's down the boulevard, bout fo blocks? Dey got an all-night guy, too. But ta tell ya de truth I think you on yo own. Close dat do of yo car. All right?"

I tried to put myself in his place, and I really could understand why he might be reluctant. Boy, was I feeling stupid. I pulled out of the driveway and began to go to the other gas station, but on the way my pride got the best of me. I knew I was going to look like a kook, and I couldn't face someone's incredulous expression one more time that night. I headed home.

I couldn't sleep much thinking what I was going to tell my mother-in-law. I thought for two hours, but nothing really good came of it. I kept picturing her face with a lot of the whites of her eyes showing when I said, "Oh, Mom, did I mention that Samson's loose in your car and we can't find him?"

We left the Dodge in the garage the next morning and drove to church in our own car. It was eighty degrees before 9:30 in the morning. Several of our friends got a kick out of our little dilemma. Carol and I asked the more mechanically inclined whether they thought Samson was in or out of the car, but there was no consensus. I left church in the unbearable heat feeling deflated. I wondered if even our garage would be too hot for Samson if he was still in the car.

When we got home, Carol started calling Dodge dealerships hoping that someone would help us at least to eliminate the possibility of escape. They were not sure, and on Sunday there were no members of the service department to say for sure.

I went back to look in the car again and in poking around discovered that with some effort I could push my hand between the back seat and the side panel. Maybe Samson had crawled under the back seat.

I could not discover the right combination of pushes and pulls to remove it, but Carol called a man at a dealership who gave her just the right combination. After he did he said, "Ma'am, if I were you I wouldn't go anywhere near that car." But she did. With a push back, a pull up, and a pull forward, the back seat was free.

I carefully removed it and turned it upside down. Woven throughout the springs was the glossy, colorful, formidable serpent whose escape had provided the most humbling, harrowing, and exasperating thirteen hours of my life. But it was over. Well, almost. I couldn't get him out of the springs.

We took the seat into our living room and left it upside down until Samson extricated himself. I picked him up, looked him in the eye, and said, "Gotcha, ya little devil." But he didn't hear me because snakes don't have ears. Snakes don't smile either, but I believe he looked a little proud of himself.

The apostle Paul promises that the Lord "will bring to light things that are now hidden in darkness" (1 Cor. 4:5)

Many of us carry things in our lives that are like loose cobras and boa constrictors. If they are not brought into the light and into subjection, they will lurk in the shadows of our lives until they hurt someone. We are the most likely victims of the dragons within us. But our pride frequently prevents our doing what is right. We think that if we just let them be, they will go away. Well, the trouble with dragons is that they love a willing habitat. Left undisturbed, they will grow and claim more and more territory.

How about you? How about me? Do we need to bring something into the light? Deal with it? Admit that it's there and slowing us down?

Is it a habit? Is it an old undealt-with sin that's still rattling around inside us? Has it grown heavy with time? Have we wanted to burst into a pastor's office or a friend's home a hundred times and blurt it out so that the curse of its persistent pain and pressure would leave us alone and we could be at peace again? Do that while the spirit is prompting you. Do it before your resolve weakens and you find yourself pretending it will go away, even though it never has before.

If we don't bring it into the light, God will, and for our own good. He has proven to be good at serpent control, and we need to trust him to help us after we are obedient.

An Otter Named Girl

It couldn't have been more than three days into my zoo career that I was warned by the senior animal keeper not to make pets of any of the animals under my care.

"There are good reasons for this, Gary," he said. "First, I want you to remember that it's the tame ones that get you. You tame them and, sure, everything goes along fine for six months or so, and then, bang, your animal has a bad day. Now that's just fine if you're talking white rat or poodle, but if we're talking leopard, wolf, chimp, or ostrich, that's a different story. When they have a bad day, *you* have a bad day. I'm talking losing fingers and eyes, breaking bones, and even losing your life. Are you following me, Gary?"

I knew enough to nod yes.

"There are some other things you should think about. When you tame an animal and turn it into a pet, you begin to feel like it belongs to you. It doesn't. It belongs to the zoo. It will always belong to the zoo, so don't start thinking any different. You won't always be working in this section. If you've turned a bunch of these animals into pets and the bosses decide to transfer you to teach you more or use your gifts better, then you'll feel like they're trying to punish you. You'll feel like they're taking your pets away from you, but that won't be the case at all.

"One more thing: it's hard on the animals when they get attached to you and you get transferred or quit the zoo. Animals do better when they don't have to make too many adjustments. They are healthier and they get along with their own kind better. That means they'll have more babies. We want them to have lots and lots of babies, so don't go making any of the animals on your string into pets."

It made good sense to me, and most of the animals in the aquatics section didn't make good pets anyway. Ivan the polar bear was a killer and didn't like people at all. The alligators were certainly too dangerous and could never be trusted. The male elephant seal chased me out of his exhibit every time I cleaned it. I think he thought his females liked me too much, and he was very jealous. They did like me because I fed them twenty-five pounds of fish every day. Mr. and Mrs. Beaver were very unfriendly and even turned their backs to me whenever I was around.

There were a few animals that would have been fun to tame and one group that was already tame but not trained. The California sea lions were very tame, and though we were never allowed to pet them, we could walk among them without any fear of being attacked. At the time, there were no large bulls (males), and all the females were sweethearts. This was good for me because there wasn't any place I could put them when we cleaned their exhibit. We had to be in the exhibit with them.

Following the no-pet rule was easy most of the time, but as time went on I did wish I could have made friends with the Canadian river otters. Otters were just the kind of animal that you would want to have as a pet. They have friendly faces and are very active, curious, and playful. Their fur is prized for its softness and beauty.

There was one female otter that was especially friendly. She would often stand at the gate and watch me preparing their food or cleaning their quarters. She really looked as though she would like to be friends, but I kept my resolve and willed to believe that my senior keeper was right about leaving wild animals wild.

One day while I was cleaning the night quarters of the otters, the chief keeper (my boss's boss) paid me a visit. He was a large man of American Indian descent. He was kind and soft-spoken. As a group, the keepers respected his many years of experience with animals.

He said, "Richmond, are any of our otters tame?"

"One seems a little friendly, but none of them are tame," I answered.

"You know anything about training or taming animals?"

"I've never done anything with zoo animals, but I have a real obedient collie at home."

"How would you like to take a shot at taming one of your otters, the friendly one? Seems as though our public relations people promised some Hollywood producer that we'd be able to bring a tame otter to a movie premiere in Hollywood two months from now. The boys down at administration said that would be fine, and I think we're stuck to try. They are your animals, so you get first shot, but if you want me to, I could get a relief keeper to do it. You don't have to teach it any tricks. All you need to do is get it so it won't bite anyone who tries to pet it. That may turn out to be a tall order, and I wouldn't blame you if you didn't want to try."

I have made a profession of rushing in where angels never go, so I said yes before thinking through the implications of my decision. We shook hands. My father had taught me that a handshake was a solemn contract, so I was bound to do everything in my power to deliver a tame otter in sixty days. When you're young, sixty days seems like an eternity. From my perspective I had all the time in the world to tame an otter. I came to realize otters knew nothing of handshakes and deadlines.

Fred told me I could take as much time as I needed to work on taming the otter, even if it meant letting other work slide. Aquatics was a large section. My one worry was having enough time to finish my daily work and tame the otter too.

The next morning I asked some of the guys who had been at the zoo a long time if they could give me some tips on taming an otter. Every one of them was helpful, and I went away with more ideas than I could try. I did settle on a plan that seemed to me to be the most likely to work.

I started by cutting back on the otter food so that all of them would be a little hungry all of the time. They were all overweight, so that was not cruel; in fact, it would be good for them. When I was sure that they were hungry, I would bring their favorite food, smelt, a small sardinelike fish, and throw it to them a piece at a time. One of the otters would likely prove to be less afraid and easier to tame, and I would isolate that one and work with it.

Two days passed and I was fairly sure that all the otters were hungry. I stepped into the exhibit and sat down where they could clearly see me from the large pool where they spent most of their day. All of them looked with interest while I let them get used to my presence. I took some small pieces of fish and threw it toward them, near where they were floating. Otters are curious animals, and they all swam to check out what had been thrown to them. They were all hungry and noisily ate the fish. Then they stared at me to see if I was going to throw more. I did, and they enthusiastically pursued the pieces of fish by diving underwater with their usual fluid grace. Like seals and sea lions, otters are a little clumsy on land but their movements look magical in water. One of the otters didn't eat its fish right away but swam with it. It was almost a ritual, a celebration or game. When the otters swam it was more than swimming; it was ballet. Their turns and rolls were a visual symphony.

I recognized the otter playing with the fish. It was the friendly female. I gently said hello and asked her if she was still hungry. She stared at me. It was easy to see that she was eager for more, so I threw her another piece. She wolfed it down, and her bright eyes stared longingly at the can of smelt. She looked into my eyes to see what I would do. I decided to wait and see if she would come closer. She did not. But she had come to land. I threw another piece of smelt halfway between us and waited to see what she would do. She stared at it and then took one cautious step closer to the fish. I could tell she was nervous. As it turned out, her fear was stronger than her hunger. She looked at me to see if I were going to throw any more fish, and I waited to see if she was going to get the piece I had already thrown. She didn't. She returned to the water, looking over her shoulder now and then to see if she was going to get any more fish from me. I decided that I didn't want to satisfy their smelt desires any more than I had and hoped that I would be able to draw them closer to me later.

The next day I was no more successful than I had been the day before. That's when I first began to wonder if I had bitten off more than I could chew. Otters are as independent as cats. It was evident that they could resist hunger. I began sitting closer to the water, hoping that they would feel more secure in the water and venture closer to me to get their fishy snacks. This plan worked well and soon all three otters were swimming within five feet of me to receive their portion of fish. I could feel my heart beat with excitement; for the first time I could see progress. They were accepting my presence in their territory and even looking forward to it.

Within two weeks they were within a foot of my hand but still cautious when they ventured near. I could see, as the days passed, their eyes change from fear to mild trust.

One afternoon I entered the exhibit and sat next to the pool. To my astonishment the friendly female swam swiftly toward me, launched out of the water, and stood patiently with happy eyes, waiting for her favorite treat. She startled me with her boldness, and I jumped backward slightly. She held her ground waiting to be fed. I decided to go for it and held out a whole smelt. She was trembling with excitement, and my heart was thumping rapidly as I reached out to her. The closer I extended the fish the more I questioned the wisdom of what I was doing. Otters could deliver a nasty bite, and, though she was not showing any signs of aggression, I was well aware that she might snap at the fish and bite my hand. I resolved to take that chance.

When the fish was two inches from her face, she leaned toward it so delicately, so gently, so carefully that it was clear she felt she was safe. Her mouth opened slowly and shut softly on the smelt. I let go and carefully withdrew my hand. She took hold of the fish and ate it like an ice cream cone. It was a wonderful moment. It was a magical moment. The sounds of the zoo visitors, monkeys hooting in the background, and bird song all seemed to fade and give way to the wonder of this moment that I had wished for for days. It was as if the world stood still so that I might be presented, at heaven's hand, the gift of a lifelong memory.

I watched with wonder as she savored her delicacy. She was cute up close and she showed no fear. The first step had been taken with five weeks to go. She ate three more fish, always being careful not to touch my hand with her razor-sharp teeth. She dove back into the pool and the spell was broken, but the joy of finally having good news to report overwhelmed me. To the surprise of the zoo visitors, I shouted "Yahoo!" and threw the rest of the smelt to the startled otters.

I ran to the chief keeper's office and said, "She finally took food out of my hand. It was great! She ate it right in front of me as if I weren't even there. She ate four fish not two feet away from me and showed no signs of fear at all!"

"You're halfway home, Gary. I knew you could do it. Your next step is to get her to crawl on your lap. Then see if she will let you touch her. After that it gets tougher. If she lets you pick her up you're almost finished. If you get that far, I'll tell you what to do after that. Good luck, man. Stay with it."

Our progress was swift now that the fear barrier was down. Her trust in me grew daily. It was four days until she stayed on my lap. I conditioned her to human contact by placing some fish on the other side of my legs from her. At first she walked around, but then she reached the point where she was comfortable just climbing over me to get to the smelt.

I knew that we had to move on to the next level and decided to dangle a fish in front of my face. She jumped on my lap, placed her front feet on my chest, and took the fish. She surprised me by staying on my lap to eat it. I fed her several fish, one at a time, and she ate them all in a polite and ladylike manner.

Otters, like dolphins, have naturally happy faces, and when they look into your eyes you feel loved. We were bonding, and I could feel a strong attachment building. I knew I was breaking a rule because she really did feel like my otter. I felt angry at the thought that I might be transferred away from her.

She didn't have a name. Now that we were friends, I felt like I should call her something. I wanted it to be a ladylike name, something Canadian. I thought and thought but nothing came. I decided that sooner or later a good name would come to me, but until then I settled for calling her Girl. After a week Girl seemed like her name, and I was never able to think of anything that fit her better. So Girl stuck. It wasn't all that original, but it was accurate.

The day after she stood on my lap she surprised me again. After eating a bunch of smelt, she stayed on my lap to groom. She licked her paws clean; cleaned, combed, and oiled her hair; and then stretched out and went to sleep. I couldn't believe my eyes. If this wasn't trust nothing was.

She slept with her head in her paws awhile and then rolled over on her back. I loved the contact and this breakthrough in our relationship, but my legs began to go to sleep and I wanted to shift for comfort's sake. It dawned on me that this might be the perfect time to see if I could pet her. I carefully laid my hand against her shoulder and slowly drew it down her back. She stirred, looked at my hand, stood up, and looked up as if to say, "Do you want me to move?" Then she yawned and stretched and walked to the pool. I wasn't sure whether or not we had crossed the next barrier, so I chose not to report it to the chief keeper, especially if I couldn't demonstrate it.

The next day I tried to pet her while she was awake, and she stretched out to enjoy it. My report was made, but with only two weeks to go I was anything but sure she would be ready for the premiere. The next day she allowed me to pet her more vigorously, and for the first time she played. She mouthed my hand, only gently. She pretended to bite and growled, but it was clearly a game. We both enjoyed it for several minutes.

You might wonder what the other otters were doing all these weeks. They had come to the point where they would eat from my hand, but that was it. They would watch Girl and me and our new games with interest, but they stayed to themselves for the most part. On a couple of occasions they stood and leaned against my leg to beg for food, but if I sat down they kept their distance.

One day while Girl and I were playing, a lady asked if Girl would let me pick her up. I told her I hadn't tried. She asked if I would know when Girl was ready, and I had to admit that I wasn't sure. She said simply, "Well, why don't you try?" I shrugged my shoulders and said, "Why not?"

Girl was leaning against my chest. I scratched her back vigorously. I kept scratching her back and then supported her with the palm of one hand. Surprisingly, she climbed on my shoulders and held on as I rose to full stature. She didn't seem panicked, and the lady zoo visitor clapped and said, "Bravo!"

Not wanting to press my luck, I sat back down so that Girl wouldn't panic and jump. The last thing I wanted was for her to hurt herself. We had come so far and, with only ten days to go, I couldn't have any setbacks. Still I had held her on my shoulder, and she had seemed to enjoy the improved view of her exhibit.

I reported to Fred that Girl was letting me hold her now, and he was very pleased. He said that he thought we just might make it. "Now she still has a way to go," he said. "We have to find out if you're the only one she will trust. We need to condition her to riding in a car. She might like men but not women. She may not like perfumes or shaving lotions. We need to see how she does when you dress differently. What you need to do is start treating her like she's going to the premiere of *Ring of Bright Water*. You have to think what she might face and try it on her; then we can make the decision whether or not she's ready to go."

The next day I brought Dale Thompson into the exhibit with me, and Girl was as tame for him as she was for me. Dale is excellent with animals and the perfect choice for working with her also. Best of all, it was fun to share this adventure with my best friend. We tried on several shaving lotions and colognes. Although she would sniff at us, she still knew who we were and delighted in our company. We invited several ladies from the children's zoo, and Girl was as enchanted to play with them as they were with her. We drove her around the zoo in my car, and she stayed on my shoulder. We got out several places, and she seemed satisfied to stay in my arms and let other keepers pet her. With five days to go, it seemed as though she was ready. But the final decision was in the hands of the chief keeper, Fred Rose. We invited him to go the course with us, and Girl was a perfect lady. She passed her tests with flying colors. He looked at me and said, "Good job. She seems to be ready."

We were going to a Hollywood premiere, and Girl was going to steal the show. I was just sure of it!

The next four days were dress rehearsals for the real thing. Each day I was more confident that everything was as fine as could be. I was so proud of Girl. She had become more like a dog than an otter, running up to greet me every time I came to the exhibit. She made me look good, and all of this was going to look good at evaluation time, which was coming up soon.

The sixty days had zoomed by. The day of the premiere finally dawned, and I awoke with a stomach full of butterflies and a bad case of the "what ifs." What if I had forgotten to think of something that would shake Girl up? Surely no movie stars would bring their dogs to the premiere, would they? That would shake her up. No, they wouldn't do that. What if some chauffeur honked his limousine horn and frightened her? That could happen I thought, but I could probably calm her down again. Stop worrying, I thought. Everything will be fine. It's going to be a super night.

I got to work and Girl was as perky and affectionate as usual. The chief keeper let me know that Channel 7 News was going to film inside the otter exhibit, which was great. Girl was used to being photographed and that would be a nice practice run for the premiere. Piece of cake.

"What time?" I asked.

"About three o'clock, they said. But I think it would be a good idea if you hung out by the otters from about two o'clock on, in case we need you."

"Sure, Fred, I'll be there if you need me."

"You did a good job, Gary. Everybody will remember this for a long time."

Fred didn't know how prophetic he was. I didn't know how quickly the tide could turn, but I would find out.

At 2:30 I saw Fred walking swiftly toward the otter exhibit. He was out of breath and looked a little worried.

"What's up, Fred?" I asked.

"How do you think Girl will act around another kind of animal?" he asked a little out of breath.

"I don't know. I never thought to try," I answered.

"Well, we're sure going to find out real soon. One of the big wheels over at the network thought it would be nice to have a chimpanzee at the news conference with the otter. The president of the zoo association said sure, no problem. I told them I wasn't too sure that this was the best day to bring a chimp over, but they said the network was doing us a big favor with the publicity, so let's just give them what they ask for."

I had a sick feeling that this was not going to work and prepared myself for the worst. Girl was getting a pop quiz just before her final exam, and in my heart I knew she would not be up to it.

Important people began to arrive with people whose job is to make important people feel important. Important questions were asked and answered. Questions like, "How have you been, darling? I haven't seen you since the Stewarts' party, or was it the benefit?" "You look marvelous, darling. How is my hair and makeup?" "I've just been so pushed all day. Anyway, darling, it's really so sweet of you to come . . ."

I stood over to the side, holding Girl, who wanted to play hostess to her visitors, but I wanted to be holding her when the chimp came through the gate. One of the celebrities noticed us and smiled. He came over and asked if he could pet Girl. I said sure. He commented on how soft her fur was and was really quite taken by her friendly charm. He returned to the group of celebrities and ended up being the only one to enjoy the wonder of this terrific otter.

The chimp arrived. Girl noticed it in an instant and leapt from my arms and headed for her pool. She entered the pool but jumped up on the edge to see if the new hairy invader meant any harm. She stared like a bird dog at point at the chimp, and then slowly, with extravagant caution, she walked between the legs of the visitors to get a better look at the chimp. The chimp was holding hands with a zoo attendant and looked like a hairy toddler out for a walk with its mother.

When the chimp noticed Girl, it screamed and took a protective swipe at her. That was all Girl needed to know that something dangerous, something evil, had entered her world. There was no love in her eyes. That light had gone out. I had seen this look sixty days before. It represented fear and caution, and I even felt a touch of betrayal. She smelled the now strong scent of the chimp and lifted her nose to make a memory of this invasion. When I tried to pick her up, she growled at me but didn't bite. I knew enough not to push her and just let her run around between people's legs and keep an eye on the chimp.

The director looked unhappy with me and said, "I was told this animal was tame."

"Yes, sir, she is, with everyone but chimpanzees. She's never seen one before, and as it turns out she doesn't like them."

He just scowled at Girl and walked away. The filming started, and I could do nothing but apologize for her lack of hospitality. *Ring of Bright Water* was a movie about an otter, and it seemed silly to me to be bringing a chimp in at this moment to satisfy a man who didn't know a thing about animals. But still, as I look back, the public probably ate up all the chimp footage even more than they would have the otter. At the time I felt that the best animal at the zoo was being upstaged. Tame chimps, as cute as this one was, are a dime a dozen; tame otters a rare delight. Sixty days of hope and hard work were trashed and trampled under that chimp's feet.

When everyone left the otter exhibit, I stayed behind to calm Girl, but she would not be comforted. The chimp had left its scent behind, and all Girl could do was look for the animal whose scent seemed to be everywhere. She would not let me hold her, but she didn't mind being petted while she looked for the hairy, dark intruder unsuccessfully. I started to believe we were in trouble when she wouldn't eat any fish.

It was five o'clock, and she would still not let me pick her up. Our bond was temporarily broken. We should have been leaving for Hollywood in fifteen minutes. My senior keeper joined me in the back of her exhibit and asked if he could help me get her leash on. I held her while he tried to slip the chain over her neck. She gave me a dirty look and then attacked the senior keeper viciously. I pulled her back thinking I would be bitten also, but she just wiggled out of my grasp and ran back into the exhibit to look for the chimp.

"The chimp really shook her up, Al. She wouldn't have done that to you if they hadn't brought the chimp around," I said.

"I suspect you're right, Gary. But she's not going to let you hold her anymore today, and the best we can do is bring them a live otter in a cage. We can't trust her not to bite someone while she's in this mood."

His arm was all the proof we needed. Down deep I knew he was right. Al got a cage and a net, and Girl was captured. She hated the cage. She paced back and forth during the whole premiere that night. Not only was she not a delight; several people were feeling sorry for her.

That night, when we returned her to the zoo, she was exhausted. She ran out of the small cage and joined her cage mates who were sleeping. They lifted their heads long enough to greet her and then lay back down. Girl laid her head on the back of a male. Our eyes met for several seconds. She looked kind again, though very tired. I wondered, if she could talk, would she ask me what the last sixty days had been all about? I wondered what otters thought about when their world is turned upside down after so many days of gentle kindness.

My senior keeper had been right, and his wisdom echoed in my mind. Don't turn your animals into pets.

I whispered, "Good night, Girl. Sorry." Then I went home a sadder but wiser young man. Wiser because I had learned some things the hard way, lessons I would never forget. First, I learned again that you can do all the right things, and things can still go wrong. I learned that even when stories have sad endings, they can have happy middles and good beginnings. You see, I will treasure my magical moments with Girl forever and remember the feel of her silken fur on my cheek and the smell of sweet sushi on her breath. I will remember the loving looks and the snuggling. I will remember her greetings and the trust that she gave as a gift, given only one time and only to me.

I gave her a gift, too. I let her slowly learn to be an otter again, weaning her gently from the constant care and favor that she had received at my hand. She learned again to be an otter. Should I see Girl in heaven, we will again be friends as before, but for now it will be easier for me to let wild animals be wild as God meant them to be.

Taming Girl in sixty days seemed at the time a hard test, a difficult assignment. That happened twenty years ago. Since that time I have seen many greater accomplishments. I have seen tame lions and jaguars, tamed by men and women braver and more skilled than I. I played with those animals at another zoo. I enjoy the friendship of Jack Badal, whom I believe to be the greatest animal man alive today and one of the world's great animal trainers. Jack has the distinction of being the only man to have trained a gorilla to perform a full act as alertly as a chimpanzee. I have played with tamed wolves, coyotes, foxes, orangutans, snow leopards, pythons, boa constrictors, and animals whose names you have probably never heard before.

As wonderful as my days with Girl were, they now seem surprisingly common. I was surprised to find an assessment of my work in the Book of James: "People can tame every kind of wild animal, bird, reptile, and fish, and they have tamed them" (James 3:7). It goes on to say what accomplishments God would applaud. The next verse says, "But no one can tame the tongue. It is wild and evil. It is full of poison that can kill." God would applaud it, but no man will ever under his own power accomplish it. It simply takes more time and more strength of character than any of us can muster under our own steam.

That's the bad news, but there is good news to report, too. God has both the power and the will to tame our tongues; He just requires that we request His services. So it matters little the evil or wickedness our tongue is enacting—God can bring it under control so that we stop hurting people. If we are lying, He will help us to have the courage to tell the truth. If we just can't seem to stop gossiping, God alone will help. If we have become used to using filthy and offensive words, He will help us stop it. If we complain too much, He will help us to see all the reasons to be glad. God can change our tongue overnight, but He waits for us to be willing.

God has done a lot of remodeling in my mouth, and the taste of poison is faint now but still capable of causing even those I love most terrible pain. So I am still asking for help. Why not join me and show the world a real rare animal, a tame tongue?

Bloopers and Blunders

In a lifetime you meet a handful of people whom most anyone would consider great. Now I understand that *great* is a very subjective term. It means this to one and that to another, but to me it means two things. First, it means that these people must have attained a standard of excellence in their field that makes them unquestioningly one of the best at what they do. Second, great means that they need to be nice people. I refuse to call anyone great who acts like a yo-yo. The best rating I'll give them is a *good* if they are rude, lewd, or crude with a 'tude (for the folks who don't have teens in their home, *'tude* is teen jargon for a bad attitude).

When I came to the zoo I met a great man. He was the zoo's veterinarian, and everyone liked him, even his adversaries. The only reason that he had any enemies was that his life was such a beacon of excellence. He made a lot of people look bad because he looked so good. Mark Twain said, and it is true, "There is no greater annoyance than the annoyance of a good example." Although he was a scholar of certain renown and he was consulted almost daily by other veterinarians, he was also a gentleman. He was good and kind. He genuinely liked and respected the people with whom he worked, and he made you feel special in his presence.

Yes, Dr. Chad Wordsworth was great. He was great, but he wasn't perfect. I don't think you need to be perfect to be great. There was only one who was perfect, the Lord Jesus, and it is not fair to compare anyone with Him because He was more than a man. He, with the Father and the Holy Spirit, is God. And when it comes to God, there is not anything or anyone with whom to compare Him. We don't have to compete. We cannot compete. But I digress.

I was Dr. Wordsworth's assistant, and I saw him diagnose, without the aid of sophisticated equipment, medical problems that the average vet wouldn't have guessed in a thousand years. Most vets would have forgotten that some obscure disease existed, and an animal would have died because they were not astute scholars with the memory and intuition of Dr. Wordsworth.

One morning a coyote was brought to the health center that couldn't hold down her food. She was terribly weak and in a good deal of distress. We laid her on the surgery table, and the doctor did all those things that you have seen your doctor do to you or your children. He looked in her mouth and throat, her ears and eyes, and proceeded to press here and there until he had checked every square inch of the animal's body. I always remained silent, out of respect, but also because he was just like Sherlock Holmes on a complex case, looking for any shred of evidence. You wouldn't think of leaning over Sherlock's shoulder and saying, "Hey, Sher, you found anything yet?" It was impertinent to talk, and, besides that, Dr. Wordsworth was always good about keeping me informed

SPARTA BAPTIST CHURCH
SPARTA, MICHIGAN

when he found something. I always knew that he hadn't found the problem because there were plenty of nonverbal cues. He raised his eyebrows when he thought he was getting close; when he wasn't, he would sigh, moan, and say "hmmmmm" a lot.

Well, after he had checked this coyote from stem to stern, he said, "Let's get her to x-ray." We did. When he had examined the shots, he frowned and shrugged his shoulders. He looked at me and said, "I'm missing something." We did blood work and the lab tech reported it normal.

We took her back to the surgery room, and the doctor spent a lot of time palpating (poking around and pressing) the abdominal region. Finally, he put his stethoscope to his ears and listened here and there. Then he bit his lip and said, just like the great Sherlock, "I think I've got it." He disappeared for a minute and returned with an old college textbook. He looked in the index and exclaimed, "Aha!" He fumbled through the pages until he found what he was looking for and read furiously. As he read I could tell he was confirming his suspicions about the animal's symptoms. He pointed to a heading entitled, "The String Affect." He said to me, "Read that, Gary." A lot of what I read was very technical medical language and incomprehensible to me, but one thing was very clear: it appeared that our suffering coyote had swallowed a very long piece of string that was refusing to pass through the digestive tract. If we didn't do something soon, her stomach would continue to retch and the overproduction of stomach acid would create an ulcer and probably kill her.

The animal was prepared for surgery. In no time Dr. Wordsworth was holding up a piece of string nearly five feet long. "Nylon," he said. "I bet this came off a helium balloon." He smiled a big all-inclusive smile. He was proud he had remembered an obscure, hard-to-diagnose problem, and he was glad the coyote was now going to make it.

On that day he said, "Well, my schooling was good for something." Then he placed his very Sherlock Holmes-ish pipe between his teeth, leaned back in his chair, and smiled. I smiled too. He was really something, silhouetted against his profound library, a library that was more than decoration. He knew what was in those books, but he was never stuffy or conceited about it.

I was also with him on a day when he didn't look so good. Remember, I said he was great, not perfect. He was human, but he was great for a human. I think you know what I mean.

One morning our secretary, Gloria Wiltsee, received a distress call from a relatively new keeper. He told her that his ocelot, a small, leopard-like cat that ranges from Mexico to the jungles of South America, was ready to "pop" (that's a zoo expression meaning *ultra ready to give birth*). He said that she was exhausted, breathing heavily, and uncomfortable.

When Gloria told Dr. Wordsworth, he turned to me and said, "Let's go. We can't keep a mother waiting." We drove to the front of the cage and met the worried keeper, who was staring with grave concern at his cat. Nobody spoke while the doctor looked with wisdom and compassion at the distressed cat. If anyone had spoken, I would have hushed them, knowing that my boss was at work and needed the time to concentrate. No one would interrupt Tolstoy, Einstein, or Aristotle.

Dr. Wordsworth asked the keeper if the ocelot was overdue. The keeper said, "To tell you the truth, sir, I wasn't here when they were breeding, so I don't know, and there is nothing in the records to indicate a breeding date."

The cat was panting heavily. She got up and walked a few steps to find a more comfortable position. Then she flopped down and began to pant even more heavily. "I think we won't wait any longer," Dr. Wordsworth said with conviction. "We will go ahead and do a C-section. If we wait any longer she will be too exhausted. She'll be a poor surgical risk. Gary, you stay behind and crate her up. I'll be back in fifteen minutes."

He prepared an injection for me to give her when I had her in a net. He then left to check on a matter at the elephant house, knowing that it would only be a few minutes.

I netted the weakened animal with no trouble because it did not want to run. I gave her the shot and watched her relax as a result of the injection. Then I laid her in the crate and waited for the doctor to pick me up. When he returned, he stayed in the truck, and the keeper and I lifted the crate into the bed. We drove up the hill to the health center. The warmth of the morning sun felt good on the back of my neck. It also felt good to be riding in the cab of a truck with the finest zoo vet in the world.

When we got to the health center, Dr. Wordsworth said, "Prep her for surgery. I need to make a phone call. Just have the lab tech come and get me when you're ready for me."

I lifted the cat onto the surgery table and got the clippers. I shaved the cat's abdomen and then got a razor. Now something was bothering me. This cat didn't look exactly like a female, but then it didn't look like a male either. I thought to myself, *Should I mention this to the doctor? Don't be silly,* I answered myself. *He knows a female when he sees it. Boy what a stupid thought. Just do your job and shut up. With Wordsworth you just do. You don't question. You don't even have to think. He knows everything that a vet can know. Just prep this baby for surgery and call him when it's ready. That's what he said to do; that's what I'm going to do.*

The only disadvantage of working around a superior intellect is that you find it easy to give up thinking yourself. You find yourself being pulled along in the wake of a great ship. Life's easy when you just do and you don't have to think.

When the cat was ready, I called him in to scrub. He was always thorough and talked as he scrubbed about other Cesarean sections that he had performed. He was extra cheery. When Al Post, the senior keeper at the health center, dropped in, Dr. Wordsworth invited him to stay and watch.

Part of surgical prepping included placing a surgical drape over the cat. The only part visible was the head, where we would be administering anesthesia, and a hole in the middle of the drape that revealed the surgical field. The field in this case was the abdomen.

I helped the doctor put on his gloves and exposed the germ-free surgical instruments. He clamped the drape onto the cat's abdomen, so that the drape wouldn't move, and reached for the scalpel to make an incision, through which he would remove the kittens. I had an incubator warm and ready to receive them, never tiring of the wonder of life and anxious to be handed the kittens one by one. The mother usually has only two or three, so the surgery would not take too long. That was all part of the excitement, seeing how many and what sex.

The doctor deftly drew the scalpel across the abdomen and blood began to seep out from the edges of the incision. The lab tech dabbed the blood with sterile gauze pads while the doctor clamped the blood vessels with hemostats and then tied them off with sutures. The skin was pulled back so he could enter the abdominal cavity. He drew the scalpel across the stomach muscles and repeated the process of tying off blood vessels.

When he broke through to the abdominal cavity, clear yellow fluid began to gush forth. It saturated the surgical drape and then began to audibly drain into the bucket that hung at the end of the table. Dr. Wordsworth said, "Uh-oh!" He stared into the lower abdominal cavity and then closed his eyes the way you might if you were deeply ashamed. He opened them again and looked at each of us helplessly.

"You're going to find this out anyway," he said, "but if you're my friends you will not tell another living soul, especially my peers. I am ashamed to say I have just attempted a Cesarean section on an altered male cat."

He looked at me and said, "Gary, you didn't notice that you were prepping a male?"

"To tell you the truth, Doctor, I did notice that something was different, but it never occurred to me that you could be wrong about anything. I just thought ocelots must look different than other cats, and I hadn't noticed the differences before. I'm sorry. I should have said something."

"That's not true, and I don't want you to blame yourself for my screw-up. I should have examined this cat myself, up close and personal, as they say. I'd have saved this cat a lot of problems if I had done my job properly. This was not anybody's fault but my own, and I won't let anyone take any credit for this fiasco but me. End of discussion. But if you could find it in your hearts to keep this in this room, I would be in your debt."

All of us have kept that secret for lots of years. It's still safe because I changed his name to protect his otherwise sterling reputation.

I am told that it is not good to leave loose ends, so let me tell you that the altered male cat survived. Why his abdominal cavity had filled with fluid so that he looked like a female ready for birth was never determined. The problem corrected itself before a correct diagnosis could be effected.

The story is not an attempt to teach something new. Everyone would agree that nobody's perfect. It's simply a reminder that we aren't perfect. If we don't think about it now and then, we tend to forget. We tend to concentrate on the imperfections of others so that we might feel a bit better about who we are and in so doing cherish a more inflated impression of ourselves than we should.

If being human means to be imperfect, then the L.A. Zoo is more than a fine collection of animals; it is a monument to humanity. Let me illustrate that with a story of my own humanity.

Two years after our attempt to deliver kittens from a male ocelot, I felt my humanity again, and so did a very nice young male coyote. The coyote had been in a fight with the dominant male in the coyote cage and had gotten the worst of it. He was slashed in several places and needed several stitches. The doctor asked me to prepare an injection of phencyclidine hydrochloride and administer it to the animal, so I did. What I failed to do was to read the label carefully. The label was important because this particular drug came in two strengths. As I remember, one strength covered animals up to 200 pounds, and the other covered animals more than 1,000 pounds. The exact difference is a bit of a blur in my memory after so many years, but the bottom line was that I chose the more concentrated solution and did not realize that I was giving this coyote fifty times the necessary dosage.

Nobody realized the mistake at first. The doctor did say, "Boy, this animal's out of it," but that wasn't odd because every animal reacted a bit differently to the drugs administered to it.

After the surgery was completed, we laid the coyote on some bath towels in a cage and checked him every ten minutes or so to see if he was recovering from the drug all right. The dosage I was supposed to have given him should have worn off in about two hours, but two hours had passed and he was still as spacey as ever. Four hours passed, and he had not recovered. The doctor asked, "How many cc's did you administer, Gary?"

"Two."

"That's the correct dosage," he said shrugging his shoulders.

After six hours there was still no change. The doctor said, "Gary, can you show me the vial you used?"

"Sure," I answered confidently.

I took him to the pharmacy, picked up the vial, and handed it to him. A wry smile appeared on his face, and he said, "This is what I thought happened. Gary, do you remember my having emphasized how with this new drug it's important to read the label because both the low and high potency bottles look the same? Well, you overdosed the coyote in a big way. One fiftieth of what you gave it would have been sufficient."

I was instantly ill. "Will it die?" I asked.

"Too early to tell," he said. "I think it has a fighting chance."

"Is there anything I can do to help it fight?"

"We need to turn him over once an hour, and we'll need to give him lots of fluids to minimize liver and kidney damage. Gary, everybody makes this kind of mistake sooner or later, so don't beat yourself to death over it. Just let it make you think twice before you make a mistake like this again. Carpenters have a saying I like, 'Measure twice, cut once.' Maybe we should have a saying, 'Read twice, inject once.'"

I apologized, but the doctor said he knew it was an accident and he'd let it slide.

That coyote didn't wake up for four days. When he did he seemed to be normal. By God's grace I didn't have to have a dead animal on my conscience, but it still bothers me when I think of what I put that animal through. It makes me feel very human.

Humanity's fingerprints were all over the zoo. There were a number of oversights in the construction that needed correction. Unfortunately they weren't noticed before the zoo was open, and they led to some very bad publicity and a few downright catastrophes for the animals.

There are rules that zoos must follow in their construction. One of them is that the fences in front of cages must stand three feet, six inches tall. That, of course, makes it difficult for small children to injure themselves by falling over the fences into deep moats or by getting too close to those animals likely to injure them.

When the zoo was built, the mandatory three-feet-six-inch fences were built, but a six-inch curb had also been designed into the zoo in front of the fences to make sweeping and maintenance easier. In the minds of the building inspectors, this changed the uniform three-foot-six-inch fence into a three-foot fence. They insisted that the curbs be reconstructed behind the fences so that children could not stand on them. The cost to the taxpayers was in the hundreds of thousands.

The lion moat proved to be too narrow. When the world authority on lions came to the zoo from Germany, he quipped that we wouldn't have to feed our lions because they could jump out and get their own food. The lion moat was redesigned at a significant cost. The work included tearing out the existing moat and replumbing, not to mention rerouting the pathways that passed in front of it.

Perhaps the most devastating blunder occurred in the bird section. It was built to face the prevailing winds for some reason that no one could fathom. After the first major rainstorm following the zoo opening, the zoo lost more than fifty thousand dollars in rare and beautiful birds. After the birds had been soaked by the pounding rain and chilled by the winds, they began to drop like flies. Most of the birds were tropical and could not handle the stress of the inclement winter weather. Some of the birds lost to the storm were irreplaceable. Most of the expensive cages had to be redesigned and rebuilt.

More than two million dollars in building blunders were corrected. If the zoo authority had tried to correct all the original design mistakes at one time, they could easily have spent two million more. During this period the zoo was used by Laurence Peter, who wrote the book *The Peter Principle,* to illustrate his thesis that "People tend to be promoted to the highest level of their incompetence."

One afternoon a female greater kudu, one of the largest of the African antelopes, fled her yard when a careless keeper left her gate open. She probably weighed about 350 pounds and looked like an enormous doe deer with delicate white stripes down her sides. It wasn't long before she was spotted running along the side road. She didn't know it, but she was headed for the zoo's back gate. That was all right though, because the back gate was closed. It would have stayed closed too, if the zoo's walkie-talkies had worked correctly.

The director sent out the message, "Emergency! Emergency! Close the back gate! An animal has escaped, and we must keep it in the zoo. I repeat, close the back gate!" Well, the security guard only heard, "Emergency" and "back gate." Everything else was lost to static. Because the back gate was closed, he thought he was supposed to open it for the fire department, an ambulance, or the police. He rushed out of the booth, unlocked the padlock, and pushed the gate open. His timing was perfect. The female kudu ran past him, and he never saw her. She was lost to the wide expanses of Griffith Park forever. She was never seen again, despite the fact that she was four times the size of a deer.

It all adds up to one conclusion: These are the acts of fallible creatures. To be human is to be fallible. Our history should be enough to humble us, but it doesn't. We keep trying to convince ourselves that we are incredible, and we aren't. We are human.

I remember the first moon landing. I watched it with Walter Cronkite. He did a wonderful job of making it special. I was certainly proud that it was an American accomplishment and even became teary with Cronkite when Neil Armstrong made his small-step-for-man-and-giant-step-for-mankind statement. I was feeling pretty smug about it all until Arthur C. Clark, the author of *2001,* was interviewed and made the statement that we ought to build the calendar around this date, this event. This was the date, he said, when man was able to break free of this tiny planet and try his wings in space. His implication was that this was a new step in man's evolution. Now we were as the gods, free to play among the stars.

What really irked me was that he was saying that man's technology was more significant than God's love. You see, our calendar is built around one event and one life. Every day before Jesus came is designated as B.C. Every day since the birth of Christ is designated A.D. I don't know about you, but I want to keep Jesus as the focal point of human history. His provision for our eternal life is too valuable to be measured in tax dollars, and His ethics have been the standard for mankind. We would be living in chaos had He never come.

The space program has brought some benefits. What would we do without Tang? We use satellites for better television reception and telephone communication. And just think of how thorough our spying capabilities are from space. Our ability to shower the world with nuclear warheads has grown geometrically, thanks to space exploration. And what can we say about the handful of rocks that have been brought back? They certainly have a unique souvenir value.

It seems to me we have spent more on space than it's worth. Considering the billions of dollars and the lost lives, I wonder if it was worth it. I am sure of one thing: It's worth cannot be compared to that which is incomparable, namely, God's love in Christ.

How does God view man? First of all, consider what we are made of: "Then the Lord God took dust from the ground and formed man from it. The Lord breathed the breath of life into the man's nose. And the man became a living person" (Gen. 2:7). We're dirt! That's what we start as and end as. Essentially we began as a mud pie that God gave mouth-to-mouth resuscitation. Not diamond dust. Not a comet's tail. Just garden-variety soil, the same soil out of which He formed the animals and breathed into them.

God knows better than anyone what we are because He made us. "He knows how we were made. He remembers that we are dust." (Ps. 103:14). I find that very comforting: He knows what it means to be human. In Psalm 103:15–16, David further comments: "Human life is like grass. We grow like a flower in the field. After the wind blows, the flower is gone. There is no sign of where it was."

Let's sum up what we have learned about man from these passages:

1. Man was made out of dirt.
2. We are like flowers and grass, here today and gone tomorrow.
3. We are very forgettable.

The Book of Ecclesiastes tells us something else about ourselves that we rarely want to hear. "But I decided that God leaves it the way it is to test people. He wants to show them they are just like animals. The same thing happens to animals and to people. They both have the same breath. So they both die. People are no better off than the animals. The lives of both are soon gone. Both end up the same way. Both came from dust. And both will go back to dust. Who can be sure that the spirit of man goes up to God? Or who can be sure that the spirit of an animal goes down into the ground?" (Eccles. 3:18–21).

The Lord keeps bringing up this dust thing, so maybe we should lay hold of it to keep us humble. He adds another little dig to our man-list by telling us that we are beasts. We don't like to think of ourselves as animals, but here it is by the inspiration of the Spirit. No amount of wiggling or twisting can change this passage in which God felt compelled to test us by showing us that we were animals.

The prophet Isaiah gives us an even broader notion of God's view of humanity. "Compared to the Lord all the nations are worth nothing. To him they are less than nothing" (Isa. 40:17). And the apostle Paul writes, "What a miserable man I am! Who will save me from this body that brings me death? God will. I thank him for saving me through Jesus Christ our Lord! So in my mind I am a slave to God's law. But in my sinful self I am a slave to the law of sin" (Rom. 7:24–25).

Let's review our list. God said that we are dirt, temporary, forgettable, beasts, nothing, emptiness, wretched, and sinful. And He means it. We need to get a renewed view of our unworthiness to appreciate the love and grace of God adequately. What of Romans 3:10–12? "As the Scriptures say: 'There is no one without sin. None! There is no one who understands. There is no one who looks to God for help. All have turned away. Together, everyone has become evil. None of them does anything good.'" And Romans 3:23: "All people have sinned and are not good enough for God's glory"?

You know what all these scriptures are telling us? They are telling us what our hearts tell us in our quiet moments. We need the Lord. We need guidance. We need forgiveness. We need help. The Lord strips us of everything so that we might learn to depend on Him for everything.

Jesus said, "Those people who know they have great spiritual needs are happy. The kingdom of heaven belongs to them" (Matt. 5:3). And Isaiah said, "These are the people I am pleased with. They are those who are not proud or stubborn. They fear me and obey me" (Isa. 66:2).

Man has value because God paid a great price for him. The price of our freedom was the death of Jesus, God's only Son. That's a high price, and God paid it to get us off death row. It is a pardon from sin, but it will not do us any good unless we accept it.

The truth is, I think we are what the real estate business would call a "fixer upper." We are a home, not worth much up front, but with remodeling and restoration, we can have an incredible value. The Carpenter from Nazareth is the best there is at remodeling. And when He is finished with His work, it is priceless. He spends a lifetime rebuilding a home. So you know it will be wonderful when it is finished. Paul says, "God began doing a good work in you.

And he will continue it until it is finished when Jesus Christ comes again. I am sure of that" (Phil. 1:6).

Trust Christ if you haven't. Gain the worth back that was once bestowed on man. Come to God empty-handed, for we have nothing but our need of Him. Know Christ and you will discover the real glory of man. This glory is that He believes, for whatever reason, we are worth His love. If you don't understand it, you're not alone. I don't either.

El Lobo

In 1966 it was possible to order a wolf pup and make a pet of it. In fact you could keep just about any animal as a pet that's now found in a zoo, excepting hippos and rhinos and perhaps giraffes. I suppose if you lived in the right area, you might even be able to order them. Wild animals as a rule don't make very good pets, but that didn't stop thousands of aspiring animal trainers from ordering them so that they might master them, and, in doing so, impress their friends.

It is for such a reason that a young couple answered an ad in the *Los Angeles Times* that read, "Wolf pups $175. Call 555-2891." They called the number and took down the address in Pasadena where the pups could be viewed.

When they knocked on the door, a man with a dark brown beard answered. He looked as though he had just arrived by dogsled. He asked them to come in and make themselves comfortable.

"Sit here on the couch and I'll bring the pups out to you," he said enthusiastically. "The mama don't take to strangers handlin' her babies. I don't want ya gettin' a bad impression of wolves from the mama. She's a great pet, but just for the missus and me. Ya know what I mean?"

The young couple nodded as the burly man in the red plaid Pendleton shirt disappeared. They were very excited because they had talked about getting an unusual pet for a long time. This would just about eat up their savings, but, shoot, money was to spend anyway. And $175 was a really good price for a wolf, if it was tame.

When the man reappeared he was holding three gray balls of fur. All of them were wagging their tails and whining joyfully. As soon as they were put on the floor, the little male made a beeline to the young couple and jumped up to be held. The wife picked him up and cuddled him against her cheek. He licked her ear as clean as a whistle before she held him out to get a good look at him. To the surprise of her husband, she said, "We'll take this one."

"That there male thinks he's a dog. Friendliest wolf I ever saw. His daddy is good with most folks, but there's a few he don't like, and they gotta watch out or he'll get 'em good. That pup's different though. Least ways he is now."

Neither of the couple was listening. They were hugging and petting and playing with a most unique puppy. The husband had wanted to bargain, but his wife had made that impossible. He reached in his pocket, counted out $175, and placed it in the smiling man's hand.

When they asked how a wolf might be cared for, the man told them to treat it just like a dog. "Feed it Purina Puppy Chow for the first year and after that just go for Purina Dog Chow. You might pour some bacon grease on his food now and then to make his coat shine, but that's about it. Wolves are just big dogs and don't need nothin' you wouldn't give a dog. Ya gotta watch them when they get big cause they're a lot of animal. That pup might make two hundred pounds and that's no lie. If you don't have him pretty obedient when he's grown, he could be pretty hard to control. He could get you in a lot of trouble. They do a bunch of teething, so you might want to buy him a gob of rawhide chew toys or bones from the butcher shop."

The young couple left more excited than they had ever been in their lives. The wife held the pup on her lap, and he proved to be a good traveler, sleeping most of the way home.

"What should we name it?" asked the husband as he reached over and patted the sleeping wolf pup.

"Something that sounds Alaskan," answered his wife, searching her mind for a name that fit the criterion.

"I read this dog story about a sled dog named Niki of the North," offered the husband.

His wife squinted, then smiled. "I like Niki. It sounds like an Eskimo boy who was brave and strong. Niki it is," she said, very proud of her husband for being so well read.

They drove to the market and spent the rest of their savings on dog food, dog toys, and a dog bed. The checkout lady was fascinated by Niki and managed to get kissed several times while she hugged him. The young couple was experiencing one of the intoxicating aspects of owning an exotic pet. The attention you get from other people is overwhelming.

Niki's puppyhood was in most ways like any large dog you might purchase from a pet store. He was bright, and they were able to housebreak him in what must have been record time, although they don't keep records for that sort of thing. His teething wasn't normal, though. No amount of rawhide or butcher bones kept him from chewing other things. It seemed that the other things were always costly. The young couple didn't have a pair of shoes between them that was free from chewmarks. Most of their furniture was either tattered, scratched, or splintered, but it didn't matter to them because they had bought it used and would replace it as soon as Niki was finished teething—if he ever finished teething.

Niki had two other bad habits. He was an instinctive digger. Their backyard was full of Niki's attempts to make a den. He seem compelled to go to den under their nicest plants. Their backyard looked like a nuclear wasteland by the end of Niki's first week. The lawn was also in great distress from urine burns. The amazing thing was that Niki had never seemed to go in the same place twice. It was if he hated green and was trying to put it out like a fire.

The young husband marveled at Niki's digestive tract. What a mystery! How Niki turned a fifty-pound bag of dog chow into a hundred pounds of waste matter was beyond his comprehension. It seemed to him that Niki should be getting smaller not larger, but he was getting larger. At six months he was a staggering hundred pounds of teen wolf.

He was playful and loving to all, and only their closest friends and relatives knew that Niki was a wolf. The neighbors were told he was a shepherd mix. One neighbor looked at Niki and said "Mixed with what?" The young wife, who had the better sense of humor, shrugged and answered, "I think we can rule out Chihuahua."

One evening the young couple needed to go shopping and decided to leave their pride and joy in the backyard, where, as usual, he was digging a den. They would be back in forty-five minutes and digging seemed the lesser of the two evils—digging and chewing. The inside of the house was still in better shape than the yard. They stood on the back porch, and the young wife said, "Be a good boy, Niki. We'll be back in a little while with a treat." Niki looked up, and his soft gray eyes met their approving smiles with love. He looked a bit silly with moist dirt on his nose, and they laughed at him and left for the store, not knowing this would be the last time they would own this wonderful pet.

Niki had dug a much larger hole than they had noticed, and it led underneath the wooden fence into the next-door neighbor's backyard. Fifteen minutes later Niki had squeezed under the fence and explored the neighbor's yard. The neighbors had a cat. When Niki saw it he gave chase. It led him quickly to the front yard, and he passed several houses down the block before the cat ditched him, jumping into another backyard a half block away. This was the first time Niki had ever been out and about without a leash.

There were instincts running through the veins of this young wolf that had never found expression, up to now. Hunting was one of them. An adult wolf may lope thirty miles in search of food in a day and not exhaust himself. Niki looked both directions and decided to follow the setting sun. It was Sunday night and most families were eating dinner. No one on the block saw Niki leave. Niki settled into a trot and the blocks drifted by at about eight miles an hour. He would stop now and then to smell the scents left by other animals, but he never turned back. Something primal was taking over. He was looking for something, but he didn't know what it was. It must be just ahead.

Minutes became hours. He had traveled twelve miles from home. He satisfied his thirst when he discovered an active sprinkler and continued on.

Back home, a distraught young couple was driving the streets, systematically looking for Niki. The young wife was hysterical in the same way she would be if they were looking for her child, which was exactly what Niki had become until they had one of their own. They were never within six miles of the young wolf. They checked the local animal shelters to no avail for weeks. It was sad. You could see that they were both brokenhearted.

Niki took a rest just outside the fence of a collie female in heat. After several attempts at digging in cement, he curled up and slept with his nose just under the gate. The collie licked his dirty muzzle clean, and he liked it a lot! It was his first contact with a female, and he wished he could get a good look at her.

At 5:00 A.M. Niki was rudely awakened by a rival suitor who also wanted to meet this fragrant female. It was a large dog, almost as large as Niki, and he was battle worn. He had scars in places where most dogs don't have places, and, to boot, this was his neighborhood.

His lips curled into a fierce snarl and a growl rumbled forth designed to intimidate your average dog. Niki was not your average dog. In fact, he wasn't a dog at all. He was *Canis lupis*, the wolf, and he answered the rival's growl with a growl so low and menacing that the intruder backed up. He stared hard and long at the young wolf. The dog's instincts revealed that Niki was different from any dog he had ever tangled with, but still this was his territory and no newcomer would get off easy as long as he was in charge. The dog raised the hair on his back and neck and slowly approached Niki. Niki's hair raised slowly, and he crouched to protect his long legs. He then assumed a springing position. Niki pulled back his lips, revealing his massive canines, and growled a threatening growl. The dog could see that no amount of threatening was going to cause the young wolf to give an inch.

With surprising force the neighborhood hound plowed into Niki, having age and experience on his side. Niki was strong; power and instinct were his shield. They blocked and fenced with their teeth flashing, and both made enough noise to wake every neighbor on the block. Lights went on and front doors began to open to see the titans at war. Neither the dog nor the wolf had yet made contact, but you would think they were tearing each other to pieces by the noise they were making.

Youth began to favor Niki as the older dog began to tire. He slipped. When he did, Niki went for and grabbed the dog's throat in his massive jaws. Niki shook him like a rag doll and then released him. The dog lay on the lawn in shock for a moment. When he got his wits about him, he exposed his neck to Niki, signaling that the battle was over. Niki could keep the female collie for himself.

That was not to be, however, for her owner had grabbed the garden hose and turned it on them full blast. Both the dog and Niki ran off in the darkness of the morning as the neighbors reentered their homes to steal at least another hour of sleep before getting ready for work. Most of the neighbors knew Sparky and his habit of picking fights with other dogs, but they had never seen him come anywhere near losing before. He got thrashed in this skirmish, and it didn't last a round. They all knew they had heard something fearsome, but none had any idea that they had heard the ancient sounds of the wolf in battle. It had been more than 150 years since that sound had echoed through this California suburb. When last it did, it had been heard by Indians on their way to the San Gabriel Mission. That night, an Indian's dog was killed and never seen again.

Niki headed west and north. He found himself lost in the maze of streets that make up the rather exclusive town of San Marino. Niki was getting hungry and, having no fear of people, began to look in their backyards for dog food. It was 8:30 A.M., and a retired doctor shut the gate to his backyard gate, trapping Niki.

The old doctor called the Humane Society, and they came quickly to capture Niki. Niki took it all in stride. The animal control officer took special care with Niki because he was not convinced that Niki was a dog. Niki wore a collar and was very tame, but still he looked very much like a wolf should look. When they arrived at the shelter, several employees came to look at Niki and argue his origins. Some thought a shepherd mix, others argued huskie or malamute, and a few expressed agreement with the officer who had picked Niki up. Indeed, this might be a wolf. Niki was wearing a collar, but he had no dog tag; a mistake that the young couple was to regret. They had nothing to tie themselves to this magnificent animal. They never dreamed he would run from Pomona to San Marino, twenty-eight miles away, so they never checked that animal shelter. There was nothing on the collar, so, of course, there was no one for the shelter to call.

Niki had a month to be claimed; then he would be destroyed. The days ticked by. He was not a likely candidate for adoption because he looked so formidable, but the handlers liked him and continued to debate whether or not he was a dog. One of them went to the local library and brought in a book with several pictures of wolves. Niki looked very much like the pictures. The employees began to lean in unison toward the wolf theory, and the supervisor called the Los Angeles Zoo to ask if someone from the zoo would please come and tell them what they were keeping. At that time, the zoo didn't have a very good relationship with animal shelters and did not respond quickly. Niki's date for destruction was just two days off. Something needed to happen soon or a really special animal would pass out of existence for no good reason. The head of the shelter called the zoo director, who had not heard of their request. Knowing that the zoo was in need of a male wolf, the director sent a veteran senior keeper out to make the call.

When he arrived at the shelter, he was met by twelve shelter employees who had argued for almost a month over Niki's origins. It took the senior keeper two seconds to say, "Friends, you've got a wolf, and we'd be more than glad to give him a good home. Where do I sign some papers to get him out of here?"

A cheer went up from the staff because they had prevented a needless act of destruction. Many children would enjoy this magnificent specimen of wolf for years to come. On the way back to the zoo, the senior keeper decided a tame wolf should have a name, so he scratched Niki behind the neck and said, "You look like a 'Lobo' to me, so that's what I'm going to call you. I never got to name an animal at the zoo before, so I'm just going to tell them that's your name." The young wolf licked his hand as if to agree, and from that point on he was only called Lobo, which is, as you probably already know, Spanish for wolf.

When Lobo was let out of the zoo truck, he shook himself and leaned against the senior keeper for comfort. It was then that he heard a gentle whine and saw Missy. Missy was an elegant she-wolf. She had soft gray eyes that smiled at everybody. As long as I knew her, about ten years, I never saw her show any signs of aggression. She was sweet, and, from the looks of it, Lobo was wondering if he were seeing an angel for the first time. He kept looking up at the senior with an is-this-my-surprise look? If Lobo could have said anything, most likely it would have been "Is she really for me?"

The senior keeper smiled and said, "Yes, Lobo, she's going to be all yours as soon as the vet checks you out." Lobo trembled with excitement and made some whining sounds of his own. Now I don't understand wolf, but I think he was saying, "Soon won't be soon enough!" Lobo held Missy's gaze, and it was clearly love at first sight. Word was that there would be wolf pups next spring.

The vet muzzled Lobo so he could give him his shots. He didn't know that Lobo was well covered for distemper and rabies and even accustomed to a veterinarian's poking and prodding. Lobo loved everyone he met, and everyone loved him. He had found a new home where he would receive everything he needed to be happy, not the least of which would be a little Canadian sweetheart named Missy.

Much to Lobo's disappointment he was kept at the health center for two weeks because he needed treatment for worms. He was in perfect health except for that, and that posed no threat to him.

Lobo remembered his brief glimpse of Missy. Every morning, very early, he would howl to see if she would howl back. She did, and they both sounded miserable. At first they only howled in the morning, but then they began to howl most of the day. You can't imagine how annoying wolf howling gets when you hear it for hours at a time. Let me tell you, *real annoying!* We heard the patrons were loving it down in the zoo. Sure, they could get away from the continued piteous patter, but we couldn't.

Someone decided that Lobo was miraculously healed of his worms in eight days. We made plans to take him to his exhibit in the main zoo. We leashed him, and he sat with his keeper in the back of a pick-up truck. He was so excited, he wagged his tail wildly and licked anyone within licking distance. I think he knew where he was being taken and was showing his appreciation.

When we arrived, there was Missy in her elegant gray glory, looking feminine. Her eyes adored Lobo; her body trembled with excitement. Lobo leapt off the truck bed and dragged his keeper to the cage. Missy stepped back, and Lobo was released into her care.

Both wolves observed wolf etiquette: Missy stood in one place, but not still, while Lobo walked around her, sniffing her to make a memory. Once that was accomplished, they played. Wolves play tag, wrestle, fight, race, and then they rest. Lobo lay back exhausted, and Missy laid her head across his neck. It was plain to see—they were in wolf heaven. A bond was formed, and they would stay together for life.

Lobo was as large as Missy from the first day, but he continued to grow. He attained 204 pounds, fulfilling early expectations.

Lobo formed another bond, a bond with his keeper, Al Bristacoff. Lobo was easy to love, and Al was proud of this new addition to his string of animals. Al set aside time daily to play with Lobo, and playing with humans was something Lobo had known since birth. Al was short. When Lobo would jump up and place his feet on Al's shoulders, he was clearly taller and sixty-five pounds heavier than Al. It was evident that Lobo loved Al; whenever Al got to work, Lobo was at the cage door whining for attention.

Though Lobo acted more like a dog than a wolf, Missy showed him the wolf ropes. She liked people also, but was not nearly as enthusiastic as Lobo. Lobo loved to be petted by the keepers and would lean against the wire at the front of his cage hoping people would lean over the rail to pet him. They often did.

It was a year and a half after Lobo's arrival at the zoo until he sealed his bond with Missy and she began to carry his puppies. A whelping box was installed at the back of the exhibit so that Missy would have a dry warm spot to have her first litter. She instinctively began to spend more time in her den, and Lobo, not liking to be separated from her, stayed in the den as well. For weeks the public couldn't get a look at these two very special animals as they prepared to become proud parents.

The night of delivery came very much on schedule, and five wolf pups, healthy and strong, were born to Missy and Lobo. Lobo was in the den, supervising the process and showing tender care to his beloved mate. He licked the new pups, leaving them clean and shiny, and then lay close to them, so they might borrow his body heat. He stayed in the whelping box for several days to help with the young. When Missy needed to rest from the pups and stretch and eat, Lobo would stay behind. He did everything but nurse the pups. He was an excellent husband and father and in every way continued to win the respect of the zoo staff who knew him.

Lobo became more special to us when the pups came out of the den. He was obviously proud of his family and more in love with Missy than ever. Lobo was always careful not to step on his pups, who were forever attacking his legs and awkwardly falling in front of him. When he lay down, they tugged his ears, pulled on the hair around his muzzle, and relentlessly harassed him—but to no avail. In fact, he just glowed as we watched, he was so proud of each of them.

Al was allowed all the privileges of a favorite uncle. Neither Lobo nor Missy was at all disturbed by his presence. He could and did play with the pups all the time. Lobo just watched, with no reaction except a wag of his tail, which of course was a sign of approval.

When the pups were six weeks old, it was decided that Gib Brush, the zoo photographer, would take a family portrait. He and his assistant came down to the yard. For the first time, Lobo and Missy seemed agitated. They paced back and forth, occasionally running to the gate to stare at the photographers assembling their equipment. The stare was intense and ominous, but no one took it seriously because Lobo and Missy had only received and given affection for twenty months.

Finally Gib and his assistant were ready for the session, and Al led them into the cage. Al went in first, then Gib and his helper. The puppies, now almost seven weeks old, were playing as usual, and Lobo stood in front of them and stared at Gib. Al noticed that Lobo's hair was on end, and he moved over to pet him and calm him down. Lobo kept an eye on Gib and relaxed for the moment.

Gib kept moving around to get an angle. It's hard to say, but I believe Lobo was interpreting Gib's movements as if he were looking for an opportunity to hurt the puppies.

Lobo suddenly exploded with a ferocious growl and bark. He charged Gib viciously, grabbed Gib's leg below the knee, and clamped down with his now massive jaws. Everyone was in shock when they heard Gib's leg crack. Al grabbed Lobo and pulled him off and asked Gib's assistant to help Gib out of the cage ASAP. Gib was pale and in danger of going into shock. He was an older man and suffering from the early stages of lung cancer. Once Gib was out of the cage, Lobo calmed down, even taking the time to lick Al's hand.

Gib was rushed to the local hospital where x-rays confirmed what was already known: his leg was severely fractured. He would wear a cast for a few months. From that day on, it was clear that Lobo was not safe for everyone, though he was safe for most. There was no apparent reason for his discrimination of some people, unless his sense of smell was telling him something we could not discern. He was never aggressive with any of the veterinarians, but he would growl at civilians, so to speak. He would also occasionally pick people out of crowds to watch suspiciously. He was like his father, good for most but not for all.

Lobo was a magnificent animal. His luxuriant coat would shine in the morning sun. He was massive and strong. His eyes were expressive and clear; his face full of character. Missy was pretty, but next to Lobo she was average. Of course, he didn't think so. To him, Missy was Miss Canada, and, in the manner of wolves, he loved her for a lifetime.

One June morning, a young couple decided that their four-year-old should see the zoo. They were animal lovers, and it had been five years since they had gone to the zoo themselves. They arrived at 10:00 A.M. and walked right in. They promised their little girl that they would visit the children's zoo just before they went home, saying, "If you're a good little girl in the main zoo, you can feed and pet the animals at the children's zoo just before we leave."

They enjoyed the aquatics section very much, especially the sea lions and polar bears. The sea lions were always entertaining, but the polar bears were drawing the crowds this particular Saturday. Polaris, the male, dove into his pool from a four-foot ledge, head first. We could tell he was enjoying himself and even enjoying the crowd's reaction. He wouldn't stay in the pool long, climbing out only to run and dive into the pool again. The four-year-old daughter was very entertained, screaming with delight and laughing exuberantly with each of the polar bear's dives.

The small family stopped at the snack stand for soft drinks and popcorn, and then they headed for the North American section. They were able to visit the coyotes, the raccoons, the wolverines, the badgers, the arctic foxes, and the Canadian lynx.

The parents looked at each other briefly when they saw that the next exhibit housed the wolves. It had been nearly five years since Niki had run away, but the memory of it was still very painful.

Their first moments turned out not to be painful at all; in fact it was pleasurable, even heart warming. Lobo and Missy were on their third litter of pups, and the whole wolf family was totally involved in a romp. As usual, Lobo was allowing himself to get the worst of it. One aggressive little female actually hung from his ear when he lifted his head. The crowd laughed and the young family with them.

Lobo hadn't been paying much attention to the crowd, but one young woman's laugh caught his attention. Something deep within him was stirred, and vague and warm memories surfaced. He knew that voice! It was still an echo from his past. He searched the crowd but stopped when he saw the couple. He looked from one to the other and remembered moments. He remembered car rides, being held, chasing balls, and especially digging. He missed digging. His cage floor was cement. He noticed that the couple now had a little puppy of their own. He began to wag his tail and whined a greeting to them.

They were, of course, amazed that this magnificent wolf was paying attention to them. The husband turned to his wife and asked, "You don't think for a minute that . . ." Anticipating his question, she said, "Oh, come on. Niki could never have gotten that big. We just must have a way with wolves or . . ."

Lobo continued to greet them and just them, while a dozen other people looked on. He was carrying on, whining and wagging his tail with unmistakable enthusiasm.

The young mother stared in disbelief and said, "Niki?"

Lobo leaned against the wire to be petted and looked over his shoulder in a loving and friendly way. She bent over the rail and scratched his back through the wire. He licked her fingers, and she knew in her heart that this was Niki.

After Lobo had finished greeting them, he returned to his beloved Missy and lay next to her. He kissed her enthusiastically and looked back at the couple as if to say, "Hey, look what I found!"

Al Bristacoff, who normally avoided the public if possible, coincidentally walked by while the couple was there. The wife stepped up to him and asked, "Are you the keeper for these animals?"

Al nodded and asked if he could answer any question.

She asked, "Could you tell me how the zoo came by the male wolf?"

Al looked at her for a moment and wondered why she had singled out the male for that question. Then he shrugged and answered, "About five years ago the animal shelter in Pasadena asked if someone could come down and tell them whether or not they had picked up a wolf. As you can see they had.

"We brought him back to the zoo, and he's been here ever since. He was about six months old, I think, when he came, had a red collar, was somebody's pet that got away. Can you imagine the kind of nut that would keep that wolf as a pet? They get dangerous. Lobo's changed. He used to like everybody, but now just a few can be sure that he won't attack them. Not too long ago, he bit our zoo's photographer and broke his leg. Why do you ask?"

The young mother didn't want to be one of the nuts who would keep a wolf, so she just said, "He was so friendly. I just wondered."

Her husband squeezed her hand, affirming her choice not to admit that they were the nuts who had raised Niki as a pet. They thanked Al for talking with them and stayed to enjoy a last moment with an old friend.

Lobo was playing with his pups, and Missy was looking on proudly.

"He's better off. It worked out for the best, didn't it?" said the husband. "Our yard looks nice, and our dog Skippy wouldn't hurt anybody. We got to have Niki when he was safe and loving. We had him when it was best for us, and the zoo got him when it was best for them. Doesn't he look happy?"

She squeezed her husband's hand and said, "Yes."

They watched the wolves until their little girl said, "I want to pet the animals." They left with old questions answered. They left with the knowledge that things had worked out for the best.

One of my favorite things about belonging to Jesus is that I have now lived long enough to believe that Romans 8:28 is 100 percent true: "We know that in everything God works for the good of those who love him. They are the people God called, because that was his plan." That means no matter how dark things are today, they will work out. Every one of our lives is an autobiography in process. We may be in a sad or devastating chapter, but we are assured that—because of Jesus—our book's ending has already been written and it's a happy ending. Think of that.

Four Love Stories

Have you ever wondered if animals have the capacity for love? I have been asked dozens of times, and to me the answer is a resounding *yes!* It's all too evident. Some people, though, are skeptical and want some kind of proof. So without shame I offer it to you.

First, let's define love to ensure that we are on the same wavelength. I recently read C. S. Lewis's book *The Four Loves,* and it was one of the most enlightening experiences of my life. Lewis outlined four kinds of love, each distinct and different from the other. First, he said that there were loves and likings for the subhuman: love for country, the way you feel when you hear the national anthem played, apple pie, your pet, Christmas music, your hometown, an old sweatshirt.

Second, Lewis said that all of us have affections. These have no rational explanations. We are just drawn to them for no good reason. He called this mother love. For example, I was told as a child that I was the kind of a person that only a mother could love. At the time those words sailed right over my head. Now I understand them because I have met children like me or like I was. Affection makes it possible for you to tolerate your child's behavior in a restaurant when others would prefer not to.

When my oldest daughter Marci was three years old, she loved older men. I'm talking seventy and above. She named all of them Grandpa. No matter where we were, if she saw an old man she would delight in talking to him. She knew no strangers and would crawl into a lap uninvited if given the opportunity.

At that time we lived on a cul-de-sac, and just down the street, on the other side of the road, lived a man who was ancient. It was 1968, and he had been breathing the breath of life since the late 1870s. Mr. Kurrel lived alone in a gray house that seemed even more gray when it dawned on you that not too many people visited there. Mr. Kurrel was a stern man and overweight. He had eyes that were filled with a mixture of venom and sadness. He spoke to no one. In short, he was an easy man not to like, and it didn't take much imagination to see him packing his bags for a trip to the hot place. He had his tickets, it seemed, and the train couldn't be too far down the track.

One day Marci was in the front yard while I was doing some yard work. She noticed that Mr. Kurrel was pruning his roses. I thought, *Anyone who loves roses can't be all bad.* Then it dawned on me, he might be into roses for the thorns.

Marci tugged at my pants and said, "Daddy, could I go talk to the Grandpa?" I was reluctant, but my Christian nature got the best of me, and I thought, *Why not? The old fella needs a friend.* "Go ahead, Marci," I said, and I watched her look both ways, cross the street, and walk one house down. Mr. Kurrel's back was to the street, and he continued to prune his roses, oblivious to Marci's presence.

She waited patiently for him to finally turn around. When he did, he gave her a stare that would have frozen the Medusa and yelled, "Get outta here right now! Go on home!" He pointed at our house, and Marci, being very frightened, ran to me. I could see that her feelings had been hurt. Her bottom lip was quivering as she ran to me to be held. "Why'd he say that, Daddy?" she asked with enormous tears rolling down her cheeks.

"I'm not sure, sweetheart," I answered. "Mr. Kurrel is very, very old. Most of his friends have gone to . . . well, they're gone now anyway, and no one much comes to see him. He's probably very lonely and misses them. When you're as old as Mr. Kurrel, your body is tired and hurts a lot of the time, so you don't feel good. He doesn't get to go places because he can't drive and I bet he gets real bored. Some people get real grouchy when their body hurts and they're lonely and bored. I think that's why Mr. Kurrel is like that."

I was frosted that Old Man Kurrel had hurt my little girl's feelings; I didn't believe half the stuff I was telling her. At the same time, I was taking some pleasure in the thought that it wouldn't be too long before the old duffer would be called to give an account before the Great White Throne for the way he treated people.

Marci's thinking, though, was more gracious than mine. She stopped crying and formulated her own resolve about Mr. Kurrel as he quietly finished his work. Day after day she would watch for him to come out into his yard to do something. If he watered his lawn, she stood on the next property over and waved. Most of the time he turned his back on her, and sometimes he yelled at her. Once he hosed her down to make her go home. She stayed with it, even after I told her that I preferred she not. I was very close to telling Kurrel off real good and giving him a few previews of coming attractions to think about, but—thank the Lord—I held back.

One day, when I was weeding, I allowed Marci to venture forth one more time to attempt contact with the monument down the street. Totally absorbed with pigweed and dandelions, I lost track of my three-year-old's whereabouts. Suddenly it dawned on me I should know where she was. So I looked up. What I saw was one of the most amazing sights of my life.

Walking hand in hand was one of the most winsome and charming three-year-olds you have ever seen (it's not that she's my daughter, you understand) and the grouchy old barnacle from down the way. She was pointing out flowers and butterflies, and he was smiling and nodding and showing her a thing or two himself. You could have knocked me over with a feather.

I have often wondered what happened that allowed Marci to turn the corner with old Mr. Kurrel. What changed from one day to the next? I'll never know. From that day through the next year, before he passed away, rarely a day passed that Marci and Mr. Kurrel didn't enjoy their affectionate relationship. He had his family keep him well stocked with candy and treats to make sure Marci had a reason sufficient to come down to visit.

The love they had was affection, pure and simple. It was affection because they had nothing in common. She was young; he was old. His life was made up of memories; hers was made up of dreams. He tired easily; she had boundless energy and didn't sleep all that much either. His life was nearly empty of human contact; Marci had friends and relatives abounding. He was grouchy; she was cheerful. To him the world was ancient, with nothing new under the sun; to Marci the world was young and everything was new. Still, it was clear beyond any doubt that Marci loved Mr. Kurrel, and Mr. Kurrel loved Marci.

Friendship was the third love discussed by C. S. Lewis. He said that the foundation for friendship was a store of things in common. He quoted William Wordsworth: "Friends are those who see the same truth." I guarantee you that your closest friends are those with whom you have the most in common. It is a love that women have more often than men because they are willing to do the communicating necessary to achieve it. Citing careful study, Gary Smalley revealed something I suspected but could never say with conviction until now: Women talk twice as much as men. The average man says 12,000 words a day; a woman may say 25,000 words a day. This is a compliment to women; they are better communicators. They find common ground.

Friendship also crosses barriers. I was raised in Altadena, California. I went through elementary school and most of junior high without a black friend because our town made a point of preventing blacks from buying homes in the area. There was that persistent rumor that if any black families moved into Altadena, then property values would plummet. I can remember my parents saying that though they didn't see themselves as prejudiced, they just couldn't understand why anyone would sell to blacks and hurt their neighbors. My father, who had black friends, told me he hated that the world was this way, but he could never hurt our neighbors by selling our house to a black family because some of our neighbors had worked all their lives to get what they had and it wasn't up to him to lose it for them. So I had to wait till high school to discover the joy of a broader base of people for friendships.

I loved jazz music. It wasn't long until I had made several black friends. Many of them loved jazz also. That was our common bond. On Friday and Saturday nights we went to Hollywood together to hear the jazz greats. We heard Ramsey Lewis, Shelley Mann, Paul Horn, and the great Dave Brubeck Quartet.

One night Danny Washington said, "Richmond, the longer we're together, the blacker you get." I laughed because I had long since stopped thinking of myself as different. We had just been friends, and that friendship had started from our common interest and appreciation for jazz.

I bet you have surrounded yourself with people who think as you think. They are your closest friends. Friendship is that love which is built on things in common. In friendship, as with affection, the more the merrier.

In discussing the last level of human love, Lewis points out that numbers are significant. Two's company and three's a crowd. That love, of course, is romance. The idea of romance is to become one with a beloved. Lewis mentioned that in friendship we picture two friends looking to the horizon, but lovers we picture looking into each other's eyes. Love's kiss is different too. Kissing Mom good-bye is special, but it differs a great deal from a lover's passionate kiss in the moonlight.

These are human loves: affection, friendship, and romance. Each love is unique and easily identified, and they are wonderful inventions of God that we enjoy all of our lives. Without love, life wouldn't even be worth living.

Eloise

Let's get back to our first question—Do animals have loves like those described by C. S. Lewis? Because we think of animals as subhuman, you might call their equivalent love something like "loves and likings of the subanimal." I saw this love all the time when I worked at the zoo, but it was never more apparent than when Eloise, a three-year-old orangutan, came for a month's stay at the health center.

Eloise had an undiagnosed rash over most of her body. She was as miserable as any patient I have ever seen, animal or human. Her illness turned out to be a type of herpes that would be with her from time to time for the rest of her life. She itched more than anyone can imagine. Of course, scratching just caused more itching. She cried as she scratched and sometimes threw herself against the side of the cage and rubbed her body against it, hoping that her itching would stop.

The veterinarians used drugs to alleviate her itching, but almost anything they used seemed useless. Only sleep-inducing drugs brought any relief to Eloise. Unfortunately, they couldn't just keep sedating her; that only created a new set of problems.

Eloise needed comfort, but because the herpes virus was very communicable, we were not able to offer much aid. Some of the staff would put on rubber gloves and simply sit and hold her hand, or they would reach into her cage and rub her back and arms with benadryl or cortisone cream. She would look at us with very loving eyes that pled for more help than we were able to give. There was, however, one thing that helped more than anything: Eloise had to have her security blanket. She was lost without it. Actually it was only a bath towel. Fortunately it was a white bath towel, and Eloise could not distinguish one from another, so we could use several different towels daily (for sanitary purposes).

When she was suffering most, she would wrap the towel tightly around her and try to sleep. When she woke up, she would drape it over her head. She looked like a nun (an ugly nun, no doubt). There were times when she sucked on an end of the towel, and when she wasn't doing anything special with it, she just held it next to her body. She was never out of contact with her towel. Even during our daily exchanges she would not let go of her towel until she had a firm grasp on another.

Eloise used towels as a substitute person, just as Linus does in the wonderful comic strip, "Peanuts." In the wild, Eloise would rarely have been out of contact from her mother, but in captivity she was raised as a human baby. She was picked up and put down several times a day, and that treatment had taken its toll. She needed her security towel as much as Linus needed his blanket. To say she was attached to her towel would be an understatement. She fell apart if she couldn't have it. This kind of behavior is an example of a love or liking of the subanimal, and it demonstrates that animals can attribute value to an inanimate object.

I am happy to say that the day came when Eloise's virus abated, and she returned to her own cage in the collection where she could play with and touch other members of her own species. The day also came when Eloise no longer reached for a towel-companion. She found that she had animal-friends to take its place. Did I ever mention I had a Teddy Bear?

Weird Henry

Affection is always easy to see. There are those people who will tell you that an animal only shows what appears to be affection when it has been made dependent on someone else—namely, the human who receives the affection from the animal. My most gracious response is "That's dribble."

I'm not sure how Weird Henry came to be employed by the city of Los Angeles, but he did and I'm glad he did. He was hired before I came to the zoo and somehow had successfully hidden his eccentricities from his superiors. I was told that he had become weird slowly. When he had been first hired, he was responsible and could handle a section (a section is a group of animals that a keeper would care for during the standard eight-hour workday—observing, feeding, and cleaning). By 1967 he seemed only to be able to play with them and feed them. He just decided what he wanted to do and did only that. It is hard to get rid of a city employee once they have favorably passed probation, so the zoo administration just let Weird Henry do what he wanted.

Some of the other keepers were angry, and some of us were entertained by all that Weird Henry got away with. (I was one of those who felt entertained.) Before I tell you about Henry's gift, let me tell you what he looked like and what he did that really bothered City Call. Henry was thin, and, even though he wasn't tall, he seemed tall. In addition to his zoo uniform—dark brown pants and a tan shirt—he wore dress shoes with white socks. He pulled his pants so high that his very white and bony legs were exposed like candles. He wore a wide black belt that was much too large. Its end hung down inappropriately in front of his fly. He rarely combed his hair, even though he kept it cut rather short. I never saw him use a comb; he just pushed his hair here and there as it pleased him.

Talking with Henry was a stitch. No matter how hard you tried, he would not stay with the subject. You would say "Hello" in greeting, and Henry would answer, "These darn crows here are hungry as the dickens." Trying to be accommodating, you would say, "Good bunch of crows though, aren't they?" and Henry would say, "I wonder if those yahoos down at City Hall are going to pay attention to what's really going on out here at the zoo." You would ask, "What's going on out here?" curious that Henry might have picked up on something in his wonderings. Henry would look curiously at you as if you should know and say, "Gee, I got to get my work done." Then he would turn his back and do whatever it was that he wanted to do, which was usually playing with the birds and feeding treats to them.

Henry had an equally eccentric wife who was very wealthy. She was so wealthy, Henry never bothered to cash his checks. He had accumulated more than a year's paychecks on his dresser. Apparently this was fouling up the city's accounting system, and the city threatened to fire him if he didn't cash his checks. He considered their threats as very suspicious and felt that they were stepping over their boundaries to meddle in his financial affairs. I know that several keepers offered to take the checks off his hands. Henry would never acknowledge their suggestion; he would just chatter on about this or that.

Weird Henry had a gift—an inexplicable, indefinable, mysterious, intriguing, and confounding gift. Most of us wished we had been blessed with it. His gift seemed only to be effective with birds, but that is the only kind of animal I ever saw Henry interact with. When Henry entered a cage of wild birds, many would fly to him, landing on his shoulder, his outstretched hand, or his head. Then they would show great affection to him. It was like magic, voodoo, and enchantment all at one time. It was really something to see.

Henry could feed large, mean cockatoos with bits of food that they would have to remove deftly from between his lips. He seemed not to care that they might hurt him. If any of us had tried the same thing, they would have removed our lips with the food.

I watched Henry with his favorite birds—crows. They loved him! They would stand on his shoulder and groom his eyelashes, never coming near his eyes with their powerful beaks. My observation of this feat led to the longest meaningful exchange I ever had with Henry. He said, rather matter-of-factly, "Crows are the smartest birds there is." "They are?" I responded. "Yep," he answered. Not wanting to spoil the continuity of the moment, I did not pursue the conversation further. I quit while I was ahead, and he didn't add anything to confound the moment. I just stared in wonder at a God-given gift. It seemed apparent to me that he could speak "bird" fluently, even if he had never mastered "human." I often wondered what his wife was like and whether she took food in strange manners and spent time on his shoulder. Foolish thought—but still I wondered.

What I had seen was affection: two species with nothing in common (such as appearance, politics, language, or habits) who adored each other. No explanation could make rational what I saw. It was beyond science, but that is what affection is. It is love without an adequate explanation, love for which there is no explanation.

Sally

I took care of Sally the Orangutan, and she was a very affectionate ape (at least for some). I had a great relationship with Sally. Sally loved to have her back rubbed and her arms scratched. She would reward you with a gentle kiss on your hand for the kindness, should you choose to take a little time with her.

Sally had one hang-up: she hated men with beards or

mustaches. Although she was normally gentle and kind, she would go bonkers if anyone with a beard or mustache came near her. Some theorized that she had been cruelly treated by a person with facial hair. I didn't agree with that because if it were true, I felt she would cower or show signs of fear. But she didn't show fear; she was just out-and-out aggressive. Given the chance, Sally would attack anyone with a hairy face. The truth is, like many humans I know, she was prejudiced. It was hard, no, it was impossible to know why she loved some and hated others, but she did, and it was plain to see.

Not only did Sally show affection to humans; she was affectionate to her own species. Orangutans are not the least loyal to just one animal when they mate. They are promiscuous—but they do have favorites. Sally's "main man" was Eli, and he was the John Wayne of the orangutans in the zoo. Their relationship was planned from the beginning; neither had a choice of mate. They were just locked up together in the same cage.

Eli was fourteen when he began to show any interest in Sally; she was in her early thirties. I always kidded her about being a cradle robber. During breeding season I saw Sally being affectionate. They acted just like a courting couple would. She touched Eli's hand gently, patted him, hugged him, and kissed him. When she finally learned to take care of her babies and they could be left with her for her to raise, she was affectionate with them too.

One of my favorite memories is Sally in a rubber tub with one of her many newborns. She tenderly took it by its two tiny hands, lifted it into the air, and looked at it with love and pride. Then she lowered it and held it delicately to her breast and patted it. I would love to have been able to capture that moment on film.

When animals love their young, that is affection. When they touch for comfort or to demonstrate warm feelings, that is affection too.

We had a troop of patas monkeys that were moved into a moated area with a species of African mountain goat called aoudads. It was a great move because many of the monkeys learned to ride the goats. Unfortunately, the goats hated that! The monkeys would jump up on their backs and hold on for dear life as the goats took them on an exciting ride. After a while the goats found that the monkeys would jump off if they didn't go anywhere, but it was fun to watch for a while.

One of the saddest things that I witnessed in that moat was a brokenhearted mother patas monkey. Her three-week-old baby developed pneumonia and died before we could isolate her and remove the baby for treatment. She carried the dead baby for four days. She held it to her breast and rocked it back and forth while tears streamed down her face and she stared into the dead baby's glassy eyes.

There are animal mothers that don't have strong feelings for their young. I have not liked kangaroos nearly as much since I discovered that they are not very good examples of motherhood. In Australia, a predator dog (called a dingo) has a fondness for kangaroo. When a pack of dingos charges a group of kangaroos, the 'roos leap for their lives. If a mother is carrying a joey (a baby kangaroo) and she feels pressed, she will reach down, yank the baby from her pouch, and throw it to the dingos. Now I ask you, is that any way to treat your baby?

(In fairness to kangaroos, there are human mothers who, with less pressure, will leave their babies in a trash bin when they feel they will be inconvenienced by the birth. Some even abort their children. Frankly, I don't understand either behavior.)

All this is to say that we observe animal behaviors which are similar to human behaviors. We see affection as inexplicable love. We see it as a form of touching to convey inner feelings, and we see its absence in the form of neglect. We see all these things clearly.

Friendship

Friendship is a wonderful kind of love. It is distinguished by having common interests, but it is the kind of love that you see least in animals because it has no survival value. There is so much competition among animals for food that they are not as likely to have friends in the wild.

You are more likely to see friendships form between younger animals that do not have to compete for food. I have seen orangutans and chimpanzees, animals that had been raised in the zoo, form grand friendships. I have seen a litter of tigers wrestle and play all day and then sleep on top of each other until they were rested enough to play again.

In a zoo where there is more than enough food for all, you will see animals that enjoy each other's company pair off and spend a good deal of time together. I have seen gorillas eating their favorite food and then offer some to a cage mate. Jane Goodall, a fellow keeper, noticed the pure and simple friendship between two male chimps that ran around together constantly. They would defend each other in any skirmishes that arose.

Jesus said, "The greatest love a person can show is to die for his friends" (John 15:13). Dian Fossey's gorillas would defend their group to the death if they had to. One day, her beloved Digit, a noble male mountain gorilla, did just that, and the world mourned his death. If you have not read the book or seen the movie *Gorillas in the Mist,* you really must do so—but be prepared to be angry and brokenhearted when you do.

Friendship is the least-observed human love. Most of us have many acquaintances, but we have few friends. Our fallen nature mediates against it. We find it hard to trust, forgive, risk, ask, or give. Many claim not to have the time it takes to be friends with another person. We compete in the marketplace and in the workplace, and that makes friendships difficult. Jealousy and envy trouble our relationships and make true friendships difficult to form and keep.

David said that his friendship with Jonathan was greater than any of the love that he had experienced with women. The story of Jonathan and David's friendship provides the perfect model for what being a good friend is all about.

I believe animals have friendships, but, as with humans, an animal is more likely to have acquaintances than true friends. An animal's problem is one of survival value, whereas humans have problems with a fallen nature.

Romance can be seen all over in the animal kingdom. Most animals have courtship rituals, and we can observe the romantic interludes that occur before mating. These are wonderful. For example, the bower bird from Australia is your basic swinging single. He builds a little single's pad on the ground with sticks and straw and then paints it with blueberry juice so that it appeals to the chick he brings home with him. If she likes it, they go to nest. It's no long-term thing, you understand, just a short-term affair with no strings and no commitment. It's just one of those it-was-nice-while-it-lasted things.

Rattlesnakes perform an elaborate ballet before mating. It is a ritual of courtship. They mate and crawl away. It's just a one-shot deal, over before it begins.

The female black widow spider is four times as large as the male, who is not black at all, but white and gold. She is a deadly huntress and knows every inch of her web by feel. She is blind. When the male comes to court her, he plucks the web at a constant rhythm. It is his song of love, and it calms the throbbing black temptress. She quietly awaits his approach. Every few steps he plucks his song again to ensure that he is not mistaken for just any old housefly or moth. When he arrives beside her, he strokes her with his delicate front leg and begins the mating process. He is exhausted after mating. In his weakened condition he usually stumbles as he attempts to exit the web. The irregular vibrations trigger the black widow's instincts to kill, and he is quickly overtaken. Without emotion she adds him to her macabre pantry of stored delicacies. Well, males are a dime a dozen, anyway.

There are some real, lasting romances in the animal world. God has created a host of animals that mate for life: wolves, coyotes, foxes, parrots, penguins, geese, and elegant swans are a sampling.

When I was at the zoo, the phone rang one day and the senior keeper at the bird section asked if we could take a look at a female coscoroba swan. These are rare swans, smaller and more delicate than their larger cousins. He told us that they had noticed that her ability to walk had been deteriorating. Now she could only stumble a few steps before toppling forward into the mud at the edge of the zoo lake.

When we arrived at the lake we saw those very symptoms. Our veterinarian, Dr. Bernstein, was an excellent vet, but he said, "I'm not prepared to make a diagnosis until we've done some testing." The bird keepers caught her and put her in a gunnysack. Her head and neck slid through a hole in the bottom, but her body was snug and comfortable inside the bag for the ride to the health center. She could not thrash around and injure herself while in the sack.

The male coscoroba swan to whom she was pair-bonded was beside himself and didn't know how to defend her. He stayed in the water off shore and half honked and whistled as we drove away. I noticed that she had her eyes fixed on him all the way to the truck, and she answered his cries with some of her own. It was very sad. "We'll try to get you home as soon as possible, sweetheart," I said as she cried on the way to the health center.

We tried every test known to man but could not form an honest theory explaining why the swan could not walk. We did blood work, looked for bruises, and x-rayed her, but the tests only served to frustrate us because they didn't provide a clue. She frustrated us more by giving up her food. I put her in a tub of hot water daily to help the circulation in her legs and rubbed them down for the same reason.

Day after day we watched her decline. There didn't seem to be any good reason for it. She looked so sad. Most of the time she just lay quietly with her head turned to the wall and her neck curved so that she looked terribly depressed. One day Dr. Bernstein said, "Boys, she looks lonely. Hey, swans mate for life don't they?" "Yes," I answered anticipating what he was going to say. "Call the bird section and ask them if they could catch the male coscaroba for us. I think she could use a little company. I bet that's why she went off her feed."

I called the bird section just as they were getting ready to call me. They said that the male was on a hunger strike too, most likely protesting the removal of his mate. They asked if they could bring him up to the center.

The reunion was classic. As soon as they saw each other they began honking and whistling and started a head-and-neck-bobbing ritual that I assume was a way of reestablishing their pair-bond. In no time they were lying next to each other, eating like they had never eaten before. The female immediately began to improve. Two weeks later she was normal.

I still wonder what caused her problem, but the body is a remarkable thing. Whatever it was that had paralyzed her had passed. These two were classic lovers. From the first day they came together at the health center I named them Cary and Deborah after Cary Grant and Deborah Kerr, stars in my all-time favorite love story *A Love Affair to Remember*. In the story Deborah Kerr gets paralyzed and is separated from Cary Grant for a while. They are both miserable but finally get back together and live happily ever after. It was just like the swans who were no less in love and completely bonded "'til death did them part."

Animals love just as humans love. They die for each other. They help each other. They mourn for each other, give and receive affection, form friendships, and like similar things and attach value to them. They love in the same ways we love. God loves them, too. His *agape* love makes the animals what they are and can transform us into what we should be. Animals have no need to improve; they don't sin. But God provides for them just as He does for us, except that His care for us is a different care; it is specially designed according to our needs.

Animals need to survive, so God created an elaborate ecosystem to feed and shelter them. God asked Job, "Do you know how I feed my lions?" God notices the sparrows fall, and He is moved by the decline of His Creation. In the Book of Revelation, God tells us that the time will come for the destruction of those who are destroying the earth. He loves His Creation, and those who destroy it will have hell to pay. The Bible also proclaims, "Blessed is the man that hath regard for the beasts." That, of course, relates our personal happiness to the welfare of the animals.

Both animals and people experience God's love. *Agape* is God's love, not ours, at least not to begin with. In the Book of First John we read: "True love is God's love for us, not our love for God" (1 John 4:10).

C. S. Lewis reveals a great truth in his book *The Four Loves*. He lets us know that our loves are subject to our fallen nature; they are unpredictable and changeable. We tire of things. Our affections change. We lose friends. Our romances crumble. He points out that when we know Christ and we own His love, His love is in a position to rule our loves. His love can put things in balance and protect our loves. With His help, we can love people. We can learn to put others first (something that seems strange to our age). Our friendships will be better and our romances will be more complete when we subject our wonderful but frail loves to God's unchanging and mighty love.

I hope you know the love of Christ yourself. If you don't, this section may seem to be religious dribble to you. I know Jesus loves me, for "The greatest love a person can show is to die for his friends." Jesus died for me and for you too. He stands by, closer than a brother. He holds my marriage intact. He surrounds me with good friends, and He fills up my life.

John wrote, "The Father has loved us so much! He loved us so much that we are called children of God. And we really are his children. But the people in the world do not understand that we are God's children, because they have not known him. Dear friends, now we are children of God. We have not yet been shown what we will be in the future. But we know that when Christ comes again, we will be like him. We will see him as he really is" (1 John 3:1–2). The apostle also said, "This is what God commands: that we believe in his Son, Jesus Christ, and that we love each other, just as he commanded. The person who obeys God's commands lives in God. And God lives in him. How do we know that God lives in us? We know because of the Spirit whom God gave us" (1 John 3:23–24).

The bottom line is that God is love. You may have a measure of human love, but until you know the love of God through Jesus, what you know is a faint reflection of what's available. If you know the Lord, then you know that what I am saying is true. If you don't, then trust Him today and be loved as you have never been loved before.

Go for It!

When I worked at the zoo as a veterinary assistant, I worked with nine different veterinarians. Six of the nine worked full time as zoo veterinarians, and the other three were zoo administrators who had the credentials. You would think that because they had all passed the same exam required for licensing, they would be similar. But that was not the case. I saw differing degrees of ability from one to another and thought that such diversity was incredible. So many factors go into making someone a good vet. I wouldn't have taken my dog to five of these zoo vets and expected it to come back alive.

Each veterinarian differed in his common sense. Each had a different capacity for caring. Each had his own standard of integrity. Each had a different standard of scholarship (I believe several of the nine hardly read a book or a journal in the years that followed their schooling.) Some were industrious. Some were lazy. Three had drug and alcohol problems. And each varied in his desire to build a kingdom or do a job.

Working for that many different vets was an emotional roller coaster for me. Having to adjust my own work habits to so many different styles of animal medicine was difficult, too.

The worst vet I worked with was a young, arrogant, self-indulgent, spoiled brat who charmed his way through the interviews, and then did whatever he wanted, whenever he wanted to do it. In surgery he would throw instruments around and curse if things went wrong. It wasn't that he cared for the animals; he cared how he looked. If he didn't look perfect, he'd throw a fit.

My worst moment with this vet came when two avocets (these are delicate shore birds) were brought to the health center by the Fish and Game department. Avocets are tan and white and stand about eleven inches tall. They have long slender beaks that they use to search for morsels in shallow water.

The doctor noticed that both were paralyzed and that several other birds of their species had died near the water source where these birds had been found. He smirked at the Fish and Game man and said, "Sounds like you got a problem with botulism. I don't have time to work with these birds, and they're not valuable anyway."

I asked him, "Could they be saved?"

"Probably," he answered.

"What would they need?"

"Antibiotics, forced feeding, and therapy," he snapped.

"Would you mind if I tried, Doctor?" I asked in front of the other men. I was hoping to shame him into letting me try while the men were still there.

He stared at me resentfully for a second and said, "You got the time?"

I answered, "I'll make the time. I'd get a kick out of seeing these little guys pull through. They're cute."

"Go ahead," said the doctor as he walked away without saying good-bye to the men.

The men smiled knowing smiles and thanked me for showing an interest in the avocets. I told them I would give it my best shot, and they said that they had a feeling I would.

A call to the bird section gave me a diet for my patients. It was very simple: small bits of fresh fish with a powdered vitamin supplement. I weighed the birds and chose an antibiotic for the treatment. Then I gave them their first shot. Feeding them was a problem because they were able to regurgitate the food as fast as I fed it to them.

I discovered that I needed to hold my thumb and first finger around their neck, not too tightly, but tight enough that they could not pass the fish back through the ring my fingers formed. If I was patient, the fish stayed down. I weighed them on a very sensitive scale and daily noted whether they were gaining or losing weight.

I made a sling that suspended the birds just above the ground so that they could push up occasionally and use their legs. This looked very funny because the two little birds appeared to be playing in a swing. I soaked their legs in warm water daily to stimulate circulation, and then I would pull their legs back and forth to exercise the muscles.

About all I can say about the first four days of their treatment is that they weren't getting worse. I hated it when the doctor walked by and gave me a you're-wasting-valuable-time look. It angered me all the more because often when he did that he was on his way to play with a young snow leopard to which he had taken a fancy. The snow leopard was getting wilder by the day, but the doctor was set on taming it so he could impress the many "girlfriends" he brought to the health center.

On the fifth day I had a breakthrough of sorts when one of the birds pecked at the food as though it would eat on its own. It did, and that was a good sign. By the sixth day both of the tan-and-white beauties were eating on their own and pushing themselves up and down, trying to stand on their own. Their progress was steady now, and each day showed a marked improvement over the next. The avocets were completely tame and ate enthusiastically from my hand, never struggling when I picked them up gently.

After ten days they had all of the drugs they were going to get, and they were walking on their own. They were also out of the sling. I was so glad my work had paid off. I smiled every time I walked by their cage. Shoot, I still smile when I think about that ten days and my little shore buddies.

When I was sure that they were well, I asked the doctor to give them a clean bill of health so they could live at the zoo lake. He came into the x-ray room where I was keeping them and looked very carefully at each one.

"I don't know if it was worth the time, but you did a good job on them. They're in good health," he said politely.

I was thankful for the compliment. What I really wanted was for the doctor to take on some of the characteristics of his predecessors. They had been better men.

Dr. Sedjwick was a wonder and a good man in every way. His motto was, "We never give up." He gave the same kind of careful attention to a raccoon that he gave a gorilla. It was always his best. Time was never a consideration, nor was personal risk. He once risked his life to save a newborn orangutan. Its mother Sally did not know to remove the placental sack. Dr. Sedjwick unlocked the door, ran in, and took the baby from the mother. He removed the sack and gave mouth to mouth to the baby. His heroic efforts paid off, and Jonathan survived. He was always a little slow, but thanks to good medicine he survived.

Dr. Bernstein was great too. He was a "hands on" vet and always in the middle of the action. One day we were treating a baby buffalo in the barn. It was old enough to be a handful, and four of us were holding it down while Dr. Bernstein was treating a cut on its leg. The baby cried out, and the mother, a very protective sort, made an all-out effort to help it. She charged the door and blasted it off its hinges. Suddenly six of us needed to be somewhere else or lose our lives. Two made it out the stall door, but the rest of us climbed for the ceiling, clambering up wood and chain-link fence until we could throw ourselves out of the stall.

Dr. Bernstein pushed everyone to safety until he had no way out. He dove for the floor, rolled next to the back wall under the hay feeder, and covered his head. The mother charged him but had a hard time finding a way to hook him with her horns the way he was positioned.

The baby ran out the door. We all grabbed something and got back to the stall, hoping to divert the crazed mother's attention. She was snorting and ramming the hay manger with all her staggering force. Finally the blows of shovels, hoes, and rakes distracted her, and she ran out join her baby.

Dr. Hullsizer demonstrated another way a veterinarian can be great. When the zoo was young there were some hard lessons to be learned. Among them was the problem of which animals could be put together in the same exhibit. We found out the hard way that you should not mix mountain goats and bighorn sheep.

Two days after putting a solitary mountain goat with the bighorn sheep, the largest bighorn challenged the mountain goat and knocked him from the top of the mountain to the bottom. That was a thirty-foot fall onto hard cement. The goat received a massive bruise that became a massive, gangrenous infection.

The infection ran all the way up and down the leg, under the skin, and onto the back. The infection was monstrous. Treatment required that the wound be cleaned thoroughly twice a day, which meant that we had to restrain the animal twice a day as well. It was a *big* mountain goat, and he was determined not to undergo the painful treatment. He seemed bent on dying and taking one of us with him. The fight for this goat's life was persistent under the kind of vet who never gives up. We won the fight after three weeks, no thanks to the goat.

Sadly, the majority of the zoo's veterinarians weren't like that. Some gave up right away. One of the vets was older, and he made no bones about the fact that he was rusty. One afternoon a black swan with a badly broken wing was brought in. It looked as though a coyote had tried to kill it during the night. The doctor came in and lifted the wing. It was a nasty break and very visible because the bone had broken through the skin. The wing had been twisted, and tendons and bones seemed to be everywhere but where they should be. I remember the doctor looking at it from several angles. Then he lifted his glasses, set them on top of his head, and looked at me. He said, "Gary, I can't make heads or tails out of this one. It's bad."

He walked over to the drawer where we kept unusually large surgical instruments and pulled out a large meat cleaver. He brought a cutting board over to the surgery table and set both the cleaver and the board down next to the bird. He positioned the bird's wing over the board and took up the cleaver.

He turned to me and said, "Would you know how to fix that?"

I said, "No, Doctor."

And he said, "I don't either. It's beyond me. So I'm going to change it from a problem I don't understand to one I do."

With that said, he quickly and decisively raised the cleaver and brought it down, removing the bird's wing.

He smiled at me (I was in shock) and said, "Now we're dealing with an amputation. I know just what to do."

He sewed the bird up and left for a meeting. I was stunned, wondering why he hadn't tried harder to save the bird's wing. I knew he was rusty, but the zoo had funds for consulting veterinarians who would have known what to do and might have been able to save the black swan's majestic wing.

As I said, we had all kinds of veterinarians, but the ones I liked, the ones I admired and wanted to emulate, were the ones who were willing to go for it, no matter what it took. That was a godly characteristic. My Dad always said, "Son, if you're going to take the time to do something, do it right and do it good, or don't do it." God's Word says: "Everything you say and everything you do should all be done for Jesus your Lord. And in all you do, give thanks to God the Father through Jesus" (Col. 3:17).

I guess when everything was said and done, what I admired was perseverance, the quality of hanging in there for the right reason, for the good cause, and then give the glory to God.

When I worked at the zoo I had a wonderful pastor who taught well and taught relevantly. One morning he told a story of a man in our congregation who had touched his life in a special way. The story touched me. He said he had gone to visit a friend whom he felt needed encouragement. He learned from the man's wife that he was at a local high school still under construction, laying tile in their gym. This friend was approaching fifty years of age and his knees and back were riddled with arthritis. He felt he was too old to start a new trade, so he stayed with laying tile though the task of bending over and being on his knees made for long and unbearably painful days. My pastor felt led to go to the gym and encourage his friend. He found him in the dim light of the late afternoon in the middle of what looked like a sea of tile, spreading tile glue and laying tile one by one.

My pastor came up behind him and greeted him.

"Bob," he said, "how can you stick with this? The pain must be terrible."

Bob answered softly, "I can't deny that it hurts a fair bit, but I'm thankful for the work. I wasn't always. I hated it for a long time. It seemed so dull and useless. I didn't feel like my life was adding up to anything. Then one of your sermons got through to me about five years ago."

Pastor Travaille couldn't imagine what he might have said and was humbled by Bob's statement.

"Pastor, you told us that it didn't matter what we did for our work, that if we did it for Jesus and to His glory we could turn it into a ministry. So from that Sunday morning until now I've been laying tile to the glory of God. It really helped, Pastor. I don't know how I would have made it without that sermon."

The pastor looked at the sea of tile around him and felt a bit as if he were standing on holy ground. That floor was a monument to God's glory. He smiled at Bob and said, "Did I say that?" Bob nodded, and the pastor said, "I came here to lift you up and that's just what you did for me. Thanks for the reminder."

Perseverance is an act of worship, an act of faith. Did you know that Jesus only attributed the quality of great faith to one person in the whole of the Gospels? It was to a woman, and she was not a Jew:

> Jesus left that place and went to the area of Tyre and Sidon. A Canaanite woman from that area came to Jesus. The woman cried out, "Lord, Son of David, please help me! My daughter has a demon, and she is suffering very much."
>
> But Jesus did not answer the woman. So the followers came to Jesus and begged him, "Tell the woman to go away. She is following us and shouting."
>
> Jesus answered, "God sent me only to the lost sheep, the people of Israel."
>
> Then the woman came to Jesus again. She bowed before him and said, "Lord, help me!"
>
> Jesus answered, "It is not right to take the children's bread and give it to the dogs."

> The woman said, "Yes, Lord, but even the dogs eat the pieces of food that fall from their masters' table."
>
> Then Jesus answered, "Woman, you have great faith! I will do what you asked me to do." And at that moment the woman's daughter was healed.
>
> Matt. 15:21–28

This woman was persistent, unselfish, and humble. As a result, her daughter was healed. She is also for all time the New Testament's greatest example of faith. Go for it!

In Pursuit of Manhood

My generation had no problem with a male identity crisis. We knew what it meant to be a man. Being a man meant being like John Wayne. The Duke was a two-fisted, independent, opinionated, hard-drinking, fearless man of his word. He was quiet but you didn't want to rile him. He was rough and clever. Animals loved him. Women adored him. And men were silent in his presence. He was kind to the downtrodden. But watch out if you were evil; he had a way of helping evil people get to the hot place early.

John Wayne represented justice, bravery, patriotism, strength, and honor. He was the standardbearer of American manhood, the measure of a man. John Wayne was different from most men. When most men got drunk, they looked stupid. Not the Duke. It was like he knew when to get drunk. If he acted a little silly, why, that's all right. Most men look a little vulgar when they spit, but not John

Wayne. He just looked like a man. Real men spit when they want. The best thing was that he could hit what he spit at.

There is just one Duke. There has never been a man quite like him, nor is there likely to be. I was raised thinking he was the measure of manhood and to be like him was to have achieved a quest, climbed a mountain, finished a journey.

Our family was the first family on the block to own a television, and I was raised on John Wayne Westerns and World War II classics. I cannot tell you how many times I saw him triumph in the face of overwhelming odds. I can't remember his ever backing down from a fight. I watched him go down with his ship, die for a grand cause, or rush into battle. He was something.

It was hard to watch him get old and die ahead of his time as a result of too many drinks and too many cigarettes. I thought he was above the weaknesses that plagued common men. He was my hero, and he beat the drum to which I marched to manhood. I sought to become a man, and the Duke was my model.

I remember the day I picked up the quest. My closest friend, Ronald Dahn, managed to pick a fight with an eighth-grader twice his size. Ronny and I were seventh-graders, and Ronald was one of the shortest in the class. He was perky though and, as the English would say, full of pluck. I can't recall what provoked the fight, but I think the eighth-grader had put him down for being short. Ronald had not come to terms with his height.

At Elliot Junior High School in Altadena, California, fighting was the accepted rule of behavior. You walked a half block to the back parking lot of the Market Basket and then waited for a crowd to gather. When it did, you stood face to face with your opponent and then called each other names for a minute or two. One would start to close the pre-fight ritual by saying something like, "Did you come here to talk or fight?" The correct response was, "I'm here! What are you waiting for?" Someone in the crowd would call out, "Are you guys chicken or what?" That would usually do it. The two combatants would start pushing each other, and one would say, "Come on! Let's do it!" The other should respond, "What are *you* waiting for?" Then tempers would flare and the fight would begin.

Another part of the Elliot Junior High fight ritual was telling as many people as possible that a fight was scheduled. I can't remember why we did that; almost every time, Mr. Roland, the vice principal, came and broke it up before anything really got started. It's possible that some would-be pugilists never wanted to fight and hoped Mr. Roland would arrive and end it before it started.

This time, when Ronny was involved, the vice principal didn't come; some fifty kids, however, arrived expecting to see a bloodbath. Ronny and Bill stood in the middle of the circle and began the ritual. Ronny was clearly the underdog, and everyone was hoping to see him clean Bill's plow. That only happens in the movies. When the fight finally started, Bill quickly beat the stuffings out of Ronny, but Ronny had too much pride to give up. The crowd was enjoying the bloodbath. I wasn't. That was my best friend in there, and somebody needed to stop this thing. Ronny's teeth were loosened and bleeding. His nose was bleeding, and his shirt was torn. Bill didn't have a scratch on him. Ronny took another blow to the face and fell down. There were tears in his eyes, but he started to get up to take some more. I couldn't handle this.

I stepped in front of Ronny and looked Bill in the eye. I said, "Why don't you pick on someone your own size?" Bill was basking in his one-sided victory. He looked down at me and said, "You're pretty close to my size!"

I stared at him with hatred and vengeance building up inside me and answered, "That's the way I see it!"

Ronny tried to push me out of the way saying, "Hey, Gary, this is my fight!"

"Not anymore," I said. "You did well, but you're through for today. It's my turn now."

Ronny melted into the crowd a little miffed that I had upstaged him. I turned to Bill, and Bill started the ritual.

"Well are you just . . ."

I violated the ritual and made my move. I cracked Bill's nose and knocked him flat. He bounced back up, and we really got into it. It never occurred to me that I could lose. I didn't. After I landed three or four more blows to his face, Bill held up his hand and said, "I've had enough."

I decided to quit while I was ahead and said, "Then get out of here."

Ronny had cooled off when I got to him. He thanked me for what I had done. I told him that that's what friends were for, but next time he had to pick a fight with someone his own size or smaller because I'd always feel like I had to bail him out. If he kept choosing big guys, sooner or later I'd get the stuffings knocked out of me.

As far as I was concerned, I had taken my first giant step toward manhood. For one spring afternoon I was John Wayne in a good-versus-evil confrontation, and I was the victor. I wanted to tell my dad I had become a man at twelve, but I was afraid he'd tell my mom and I'd get the standard You-don't-have-to-fight-to-be-a-man lecture that I had heard twice the year before. Lest you think that I was a regular schoolyard fighter, I had a relatively short career of only three fights: twice in the sixth grade and once in the seventh behind the Market Basket. My lifetime record was 2–1.

I slept well the night after Ronny and Bill's melee and enjoyed the praise that came with dumping on an eighth grader. The good feeling didn't last though; even as a seventh grader I knew that I had not established my manhood. There would always be someone whom I couldn't beat, and my manhood would be subject to my ability to win.

I began to wonder if maybe manhood was fearlessness or standing in the face of fear rather than a favorable won-lost ratio. As time went on, I accepted that as the essence of John Wayne's manhood.

From the seventh grade on to adulthood I periodically tried to establish my manhood. During my high school years, I drove cars much too fast and took chances that could have cost my life or someone else's. My problem was how I handled my successes at surviving the risks I took. Each victory meant that I would have to kick it up a notch to prove something more. There never seemed to be a point at which I could say with confidence, "I'm a real man now."

I received Christ at age fifteen, but no one told me what it was to be a Christian man, so I kept my John Wayne mentality. Fearlessness remained my standard.

At twenty-one, on a camping trip, my close friend and comrade in adventure, Sonny Salsbury, challenged me to a contest of sorts. We were at a lake where a cliff overhung a crystal blue pool. There were ledges that offered opportunities to dive from either twenty, forty, or sixty feet into the cool deep water. When you looked up, those heights didn't seem that big a deal, so I accepted Sonny's I-will-if-you-will offer.

We rock-climbed part of the way up and then pulled ourselves hand-over-hand up a rope that someone had installed long ago, enabling visitors to share the adventure of diving from the ledges. We had dived easily from twenty several times, so we climbed on up to forty. Using the rope, we inched our way out to the ledge and then threw the rope back to where others could use it for their ascents.

I was shocked when I looked down. The pool was at least fifty feet in diameter, but from forty feet there was suddenly some question whether we might hit the shore on the other side if we dived with too much enthusiasm. A strong wind might blow you into the trees. I was immediately grieved that I had made any deal involving a jump from forty feet. My only hope was that Sonny would offer to call the whole thing off when he considered the catastrophic possibilities. My hopes were dashed when he yelled, "Here I go!" and leapt out into space. He fell quickly and disappeared into the gorgeous blue water. He made an enormous splash and the foam kept him hidden for several seconds. I began to think he was hurt and not coming up, but he reappeared and yelled, "Yahoo!" He looked up at me on the ledge and called out, "You'll love it! It was great! Go for it, Gare!" (Sonny calls me "Gare.")

"Sonny, this is higher than I thought. I'm not going to enjoy it. I promise," I called back to him. I was hoping he would let me off the hook because of the note of desperation in my voice.

"You'll have to jump," he shouted. "We made a deal, and nobody is going to throw you the rope to get back. You'll either jump or be there for the rest of your life." Sonny wore a sadistic grin on his face and looked a bit like Jack Nicholson when he said that.

There were high school students present from the camp where we were counselors, so I decided against groveling. I thought a fetal position would be good, but the ledge was too narrow. I looked down thinking someone had done something to the pool, because it seemed farther away than when I had first looked. I knew Sonny, and I knew there was only one way down. I wanted to get it over with. I clenched my teeth and counted to three. I rocked back and forth as I, with all the determination I could muster, said, "One, two, three . . ." I'm not sure what went wrong, but I was still on the ledge. I was rocking, but I didn't jump.

Sonny was enjoying my plight much too much. That provided just enough I'll-show-you incentive. I began again: "One, two, *three* . . . four, five, six . . . oh, shoot!" I just couldn't do it. What was I afraid of? That was a stupid question; I could answer that very quickly: *death, pain, belly flop* (a forty-foot belly flop! Waaahh!), *falling and drowning at the bottom of a pool.*

"Sonny, get me that rope!"

"No, nope, never, nyet, uh-uh, not now, not later! We made a deal! I did it, now you do it!"

That was the last time I ever made a deal like this. "One, two, three, four . . . , oh, brother!"

Now what made this whole thing worse was that a sophomore from a local Fresno high school was diving from the ledge twenty feet *above* me. He was doing flips, and doing them at the rate of about one every ten minutes. Every time he made the climb he would, when he reached my level on the rope, encourage me with a cheerful, "Hey, you can do it, big fella." Little show off! What would you expect from a sophomore? The dictionary defines sophomoric as feeling that someone has arrived. Thought he was hot stuff, diving from sixty feet and doing flips. He made it look so easy and, conversely, made me look so bad.

I stood on that ledge for two hours. My bare feet were sore and my legs were wobbly. You're probably wondering if I jumped. Well, I did . . . finally. I suppose you want to know what made me do it.

The time to return to camp came, and Sonny and all of the high schoolers gathered all of their beach towels and belongings and were just standing on the shore looking up. They were tired and hungry and, from their perspective, could not understand my reluctance.

They had stopped encouraging me. The tone was more come-on-Gare-we-want-to-go-now. Now!

I looked down. "One, two, *three,*" I blurted and then leaned. My body tipped forward, and I could feel my momentum carrying me to the point of no return. I was committed! I was falling! I could feel the acceleration. It was incredible! I could feel the adrenaline in my system, and my heart began to pound so hard that I thought it would jump out. The water rushed up at me at a threatening pace and then, suddenly, I was plunging to a depth of fourteen feet in the cool blue water. My feet hit the bottom of the pool and I pushed off to head for the surface.

The small crowd was cheering wildly and for just a moment I felt like a real man. I wondered if the Duke had done this; then I remembered he'd done it from horses lots of times and from greater heights. Oh, bother.

Was I ever to become a *real* man? Maybe not. At twenty-three I began my career at the Los Angeles Zoo. I was still in search of manhood. Something told me I was going to find it there. There were a thousand dangers to confront at the zoo. Facing any one of them would surely be the rite of passage that would turn an old boy into a man. I didn't want to be Peter Pan and never grow up, but I still didn't know how.

I have always had good reflexes, and I became adept at animal capture from the beginning. I remember the first time I was invited to participate in a capture. The coyotes needed their distemper shots, and that required netting. The net looked like a giant butterfly net and it was heavy. It was made of steel tubing with a two-foot hoop on the end. The net was attached to the hoop and covered with a rubber hose so that the steel bar would not injure the animal.

Two of us went into the cage with five coyotes, one of which (and I didn't know which one) was terribly vicious. A capable keeper had tried to net him just days before, and the wily male jumped up a wall and leapt right into the keeper's face and bit him good. His wound required dozens of stitches, and he had a facial scar for the rest of his life. Netting coyotes was no parlor game. My first day of netting went well; that is, it went without incident. I had the knack, and I had the nerve. I thought the zoo was going to be fun!

When I was transferred to the health center, animal capture became one of my main responsibilities. It was my job to restrain the sick or injured animals for the veterinarian so that he could give them clinical examinations. Day after day I had to put my hands and body on the line for the sakes of the vet and the animals. I always worked with good men, so my injuries were minimal during the first three years (though I had some first-rate close calls).

One day I served above and beyond the call of duty. Jeannie, our largest and meanest female chimp, finally finished a project she had obviously been working at for a long time. She had been worrying a section of the chain-link fencing that made up her cage at the zoo health center and finally broke the weld loose. She bent it apart and pulled one strand of the wire through until there was a tear in the fence. She crawled out with three other chimps.

Jim Post was feeding inside the cage room when he turned to see that he was surrounded by four escaped chimps, two of them extremely dangerous. Jeannie and Toto had both taken fingers off of people and could explode with rage without warning. Jim kept his cool. He walked slowly and deliberately to the cage room door and let himself out. He closed the door behind him, locking the escaped chimps in the cage section. Jim then ran to inform me that the chimps were out.

The chimps were also a danger to other animals; we were keeping several vulnerable species in the health center. Dr. Gale was the only vet at the zoo that day, but that was fine with me because he was the best man at the zoo at animal capture. He was fearless.

I started preparing capture darts knowing that they would be needed. I fixed six darts, each with enough medication to bring down a 120-pound animal. I figured that we could shoot the chimps from outside the cage room, through the chain-link fence that surrounded it. When Dr. Gale got there, that's exactly what we tried to do. As soon as the chimps saw the capture gun, they hid behind anything and everything they could find. We weren't able to attempt a single shot; chimps hated the capture gun.

Several men had now arrived at the health center, watching the crisis and standing by for orders if they were needed. Chimps are four to six times as strong as a man; they were too much animal to try to net, so the capture guns were the only hope we had.

Dr. Gale studied the situation for a long time. He said, "We have to go in." He looked me right in the eye and said, "Who's going in with me?"

"I'm in," I said.

I can remember thinking that this was the crisis for which I had been waiting a long time. This would be the measure of my manhood. I felt like I was in a Western movie and I'd just joined the hero in a life-or-death struggle. Another keeper, Tony Campo, volunteered too, and we handed him the rifle. Dr. Gale and I took pistol versions of the capture gun and asked Tony to let us take our shots and then back us up. That meant if we shot and only made a chimp angry enough to charge us, Tony was supposed to threaten it with the rifle and shoot if he had to in order to protect us.

Dr. Gale unlocked the door; the chimps went crazy. They screamed at the tops of their lungs, letting us know they were not happy about seeing guns. They stayed behind their barriers. Our maneuvering for shooting position was like a game of chess. Dr. Gale would send me one way and he would go another, but the chimps refused to give us a clear shot.

Even though I was afraid, I was glad that I had volunteered. I glanced at the men outside the cage and thought, maybe for the first time, *the real men are in here.*

I finally got a clear shot. I took aim at Jeannie's hind quarter and pulled the trigger. Whoosh . . . the dart found its mark in the largest section of her thigh. She looked *very* angry and began to run toward me. Dr. Gale and Tony rushed to my aid, and we all pointed our guns at the charging chimp. Seeing our weapons, she thought better of her actions and retreated.

Dr. Gale said, "Let's hold off a bit and see if she goes down. It'll be better odds for us if she does."

We retreated to the gate. I reloaded my gun with another capture dart and cocked it so a blast of CO2 filled the cartridge.

Dr. Gale said, "Nice work, Richmond. You held your ground good in there."

"Thanks for the back up," I said. "I think she would have been all over me if you guys hadn't been there."

"No problem. Just do the same for us if we need it."

I nodded, hoping I'd have the nerve to stand my ground as they did. We walked back in the cage room, and Jeannie was down for the count. She was lying flat on her back, sound asleep. Next to her was the capture dart that she had pulled out and dropped to the concrete.

Three chimps to go.

There was an empty cage, and Dr. Gale opened the door.

"Let's not make this any harder than we have to," he said. "Maybe we'll get lucky and be able to scare one or two in here."

We jockeyed for position with the other chimps and were able to get Toto in front of the open cage. To our surprise he ran in, jumped up on the seating bench, and whimpered and shook his hands. He was expressing his fear. We shut the door behind him and had only two chimps to go, neither of which was very aggressive.

The two remaining fugitives were females, both fairly gentle. Still they were agitated and could not be led safely to a cage. They had to be darted.

Dr. Gale made a perfect shot on Annie. After she went down, I got Bonnie. I can't describe my sense of relief; nor can I tell you how like a man I felt. That was hazardous duty, and I knew it. There was a lot of back patting, and it felt good. I felt like a real man—well, at least for awhile.

Not too long after that, the reptile house called to let us know that they had an emergency. One of the residents was a species of python that lays its eggs and then stays around to incubate them. This is very rare among reptiles. Alligators and crocodiles incubate their eggs, but snakes very rarely have this instinct. In this instance, this species of python not only stays with its eggs, but it twitches regularly so it can actually raise its body temperature.

The problem at the reptile house was that a particular female had laid her eggs on some gravel and twitched the gravel away, exposing a heating element. Dedicated mother that she was and also having a high threshold for pain, she remained on the heating element until the reptile keepers smelled burning snake. When they removed her from the cage, they discovered that she had burned a hole six inches wide through her belly.

The keepers carefully removed the eggs (there were about thirty) and brought the mother and eggs to the health center. We treated her burn, but the injury was so bad she would need daily attention.

Now this was a big snake. She was fourteen feet long and capable of killing a man. We put her in a box four feet by four feet in the pharmacy and returned her eggs to her. It was a glad reunion. She nuzzled each one, scooted them into a fine little pile, and then encircled them. When she began her rhythmic twitching, we all believed that there was still a chance that her babies would be saved.

Snakes have a slow metabolism, so everything about them happens slowly. They move slowly, digest slowly, and (important to this story) heal slowly.

This gigantic mother python went back to her routine of pulsating incubation. At the same time, we needed to clean her wound and change her dressing every three days. Now this was no easy task because she was a mother on a mission. Whenever we removed the lid from her cage, her impression was that we were after her eggs.

Now the Lord gave this serpent an above-average mothering instinct, and I'm here to tell you that she made helping her a chore. She would turn toward anyone who got near her and hiss with rage. She postured in a striking position, and the reptile keepers in charge of restraining her for us would have to jockey for position a bit before they made their lunge.

These guys, especially Jay Kilgore, were good and never missed. Jay would grasp her firmly behind the head and the rest of us would control the body so the doctor could treat the wound. If Jay miscalculated—even a little —he would end up with rows of massive teeth deeply sunk into his hand. She was not a poisonous snake, but her bite would be both painful and dirty. Snakes regularly shed their teeth, so you could be sure that several of hers would break off in the wound and cause massive infections. She was a handful, and I admired the men who made the grab.

I asked the reptile keepers if I could make the head grab the next time she needed her treatment. I needed to turn my adventure quotient up a notch, and this appeared to be a good time to do it.

Two days later the men arrived and again I asked if I could make the head grab. They were more than willing to let me have a go at it. In fact, they were very encouraging. They said that there was nothing to it. Jay coached me, pretending my arm was her neck and my hand was her head. He told me that I might be a little surprised by her strength and to hold on tight or I would surely get nailed and probably get the other keepers nailed also.

We removed the lid from the cage, and she became tense and alert. She turned her head so that she could see her adversaries one by one. I felt numb when she stared at me. Like Jay, I moved about to confuse her and get into a position to make the grab. My moment came. She was looking away at another keeper. Now was the perfect time. Unlike my lake jump, there was no room for counting. In this business you just reacted because you were dealing with animals that reacted—and reacted quickly.

Unfortunately, I couldn't. I froze. My mind was screaming *grab,* but my body was saying *No way, get us out of here.* My body won and suddenly the moment was gone. The python turned and stared directly into my eyes. Everything about her said, "I dare you."

The reptile guys said, "Why don't you watch us another day? You can pick it up later. It's cool. We can't grab wolves and cheetahs and baboons, so don't feel bad about this."

I backed off. I felt stripped of my manhood. John Wayne would have grabbed her, but I couldn't. I never did.

Big, *really* big, snakes seem to bother me. I recently owned a nine-foot Burmese python that I named Jabba. I was able to grab him okay. He bit me one day when I was trying to feed him, but it wasn't personal. He was aiming for his food and missed. I sold him the next week. I still could not grab the female in this story.

I was nearly thirty when it dawned on me that if I continued to hold onto my definition of manhood I would always be a boy. There was always going to be one more mountain to climb, and, with my tendency to volunteer, sooner or later I was going to fall real good! I remember one day looking at my hands and thinking, *Listen, Bud, you still have all your fingers and you haven't been mauled. There are no big holes where horns have been jammed through you, so why don't you back off and let the younger guys chase manhood for awhile?*

You know, I did. Whenever the opportunity to volunteer for dangerous duty came up, I started keeping my hands in my pockets. If I couldn't find manhood for seven years on that path, I would look for it somewhere else. You wouldn't believe how many guys came forward to take my place. They never found their manhood, but I did.

The One who designed us has written things about what it means to be men and women, but I had never noticed them before. I soon discovered that the things in life that matter included unselfish heroics, but foolish heroics didn't appear anywhere on the list. This list started with those things that had to do with good character: kindness, honesty, unselfishness, and integrity. Nowhere in the Scripture is manhood more clearly defined than in Micah 6:8:

> The Lord has told you what is good.
> He has told you what he wants from you:
> Do what is right to other people.
> Love being kind to others.
> And live humbly, trusting your God.

And in Ecclesiastes, I found:

> Now, everything has been heard.
> Here is my final advice:
> Honor God and obey his commands.
> This is the most important thing people can do.
> God knows everything people do,
> even the things done in secret.
> He knows all the good and all the bad.
> He will judge everything people do.
>
> Eccles. 12:13–14

The prophet Isaiah certainly affirms this assessment. There God says, "These are the people I am pleased with. They are those who are not proud or stubborn. They fear me and obey me" (Isa. 66:2).

Heroics have their place. Jesus said in John 15:13: "The greatest love a person can show is to die for his friends." Jesus wasn't talking about the kind of Evel-Knievel heroics I aspired to all of my life; He was talking about bravery for the sake of others, not to prove something but to act as an expression of an inward reality. He was talking about bravery as a byproduct of love.

With God, our character is always paramount. That's why He set aside Moses when he was at his John Wayne best and sent him to the wilderness for forty years to straighten out his character. It was well worth the time: God said later, "There is none like my servant Moses."

Pontius Pilate didn't know it, but when he brought Jesus before the people and said, "Here is the man!" (John 19:5), he was introducing everything God intended a man to be. Jesus is a man's man and the ideal man for women because He was brave and good and kind. He was also the greatest example of unselfishness that the world has ever known. Now I want to be like Him.

Keeping Your Head above Water

Henry was a sloth bear. Now describing a sloth bear is no simple task, but if you can imagine a bear made out of assorted spare bear parts, you might start to get the picture. Sloth bears are on the small side, weighing not more than 200 pounds. They are bushy all over, particularly around the head. When you look at a sloth bear, you might feel reluctant to ascribe its origin to one of the six days of Creation. Once you've seen one, you might think that way back at the beginning of time a black male lion had married a small female bear. (Maybe the lion had very poor eyesight and the she-bear never bothered to mention that she was a bear.) As a matter of fact, sloth bears look more like something that happened to a bear.

Sloth bears are mostly black, with just a touch of white or gray around their muzzles, but that mostly depends on their age. Tufts of hair stick up from the ends of their saggy ears. And they are pigeon-toed; they rock back and forth when they walk.

Henry was a prime specimen of sloth bear, but he was also a little more than that. Henry's behavior was as bizarre as bears get. He had several quirks that made him memorable. To give you some idea of how special Henry was, consider this. The zoo owned sixteen bears that represented six different species, but only two were named: Ivan, the 950-pound polar bear, and little Henry, the eccentric sloth bear. Henry threw tantrums. He threw them all the time, and he didn't require much of a reason. Flies buzzing around his head might set him off. Being denied a treat after he had begged for food might do it. Being let in for dinner two minutes late was a sure bet.

You know the expression, "You're acting like a real bear"? The first time they used it, they put Henry's picture next to it—not a full body shot but a close-up of his face. It made you wonder why they named him Henry, unless he was named for Henry VIII. I would have chosen the name Grumpy.

As grouchy as Henry was, you couldn't help but like the little fellow, because he was possessed of the same mettle as Snow White's Grumpy. I saw him as stout-hearted and brave, and it hurts to tell you his story.

Henry had a lot of bad days; he liked it that way. But he liked making them bad himself. One dreary January day, after it had rained for several days, Henry spent the worst day of his life.

Henry's bear moat was constructed below the level of the surrounding drainage system. When water ran into the moat or the surrounding drains they would begin to fill until a float activated a pump that would drain the excess water away. The drains had always worked faithfully, and it never occurred to anyone that one night they would not. The ground was fully saturated and the torrents of water were cascading from the adjacent hillsides as the rain challenged the hillsides with relentless fury.

The pumps had worked overtime for several days in a row, and their strength was failing. Their time was silently at hand. That night as Henry's keeper George left to go home, he could not foresee the nightmare he would face the next morning. He smiled at Henry, who had just come off exhibit and was already busy sifting through a pile of delicacies that George had lovingly prepared minutes before. Henry didn't look up when George said good night. It wasn't his way. But this was always the one moment each day when Henry was incapable of hiding his capacity for joy. He loved food, and he didn't care who knew it. The last sounds George heard as he closed the back door of the bear grotto were Henry's ecstatic utterances, spontaneously generated while eating his favorite foods.

When George left, Henry ate and ate until his floor was completely free from any small bit of food. He then licked his paws clean and circled his grotto until he was ready to lie down for the night. Sleep came quickly to a mind with no cares. In no time Henry was snoring and dreaming of more treats and faraway Eastern jungles with exotic vines and flowers.

Henry was completely unaware that the pump had broken and that the water in his moat was rising at an alarming rate. He did not realize that before morning his grotto could be his tomb. He was surrounded by concrete and steel, and there was no way of escape.

It wasn't until three o'clock in the morning that Henry was awakened by water that was licking at his right paw, which was dangling from his sleeping platform. He stood and viewed something he was still unable to understand. His cage was filling with water. By 3:30 that morning the water had risen to his belly. Nobody was there to see it, but I'm sure Henry threw a tantrum—a first-class tizzy. He probably began by jumping up and down on his front feet. Then in full bad humor, he jumped up and down on all fours. It didn't do any good though, because the water kept rising and was now up to his neck. I believe his instincts to survive were now stimulated and he would have paced with his head high. Minutes later Henry was beyond pacing. He was forced to do what all bears can do so well, stand up. All bears can do it but never have to do it for very long; it just isn't comfortable. Comfort was no longer an option. It was stand or die and the water was still rising.

The only light in the bear grotto was a 25-watt bulb mounted near the ceiling. It cast an eerie light that danced dimly across the water to Henry. Henry looked at the back door, which was now four feet deep in water, and wished that George would come through and let him out on exhibit where he could crawl to higher ground. It was now 4:30 in the morning and it would be nearly four hours before keepers began to arrive at the zoo to check on their animals. Henry didn't have that much time. The water was now up to his mouth, and he was standing on his tiptoes to breathe. He still watched the door for George's appearance and moaned sadly because he was afraid. Being a tropical bear, he was not enjoying the cold water that engulfed him. Minutes must have seemed like hours to this frightened little sloth bear. The water had risen even more, and Henry was dancing to keep his head above water. The rain kept coming, and there was no evidence it would stop. The gully where Henry lived looked like a small lake, even outside the grotto. Security knew the tunnel leading to Henry's area was filling up with water, but it did not occur to them that the bear moat was filling up also. No emergency plan was put into action; security thought that maintenance could deal with a plugged drain tomorrow.

When George arrived at the zoo the next morning, he frowned at the perilous gray sky and pulled his rain gear closer to his body as he got out of his car. The rain was coming down harder than ever and stung his face and hands as he walked toward his section. He stopped to chat with Bob Morris, the aquatics keeper, who asked if maybe it was time to start thinking about building an ark. George said he didn't think that was such a far-out idea in light of the number of days in a row that it had rained. They exchanged small talk; then George walked briskly to his section. When he got to the tunnel and saw that it was waist deep in water, George's heart began to pound. He yelled "HENRY!" and waded through the waist-deep water to the bear moat. A feeling of hopelessness overwhelmed him when he saw the lake that surrounded the bear moat. It was deep, and in George's mind Henry was history. George waded into the icy water and made his way to the back door of the bear's moat. He reached under the water, opened the door, and waded inside. The 25-watt bulb, still working, offered dim light. As George's eyes adjusted, he was able to see something his mind could not comprehend. There were both of Henry's paws reaching as high as they could reach, and more importantly, George could see Henry's nose, about four inches of it, sticking above the water. George was struck silent. And during that silence, he could hear Henry's systematic, rhythmic breathing. It was obvious that he was able to breathe only through his nose. George yelled, "Henry, hang on!" then ran for a telephone.

"Security, call maintenance and tell 'em to bring every pump they have, quickly, or we're going to lose a sloth bear. His moat is filled with water. There isn't a moment to spare. Help me!"

Security got right on it, and soon several maintenance men were busy setting pumps and firing them up. Although he was shivering, George stood chest deep in water to watch his bear. He hoped Henry would survive.

George stared at Henry's nose and thought maybe there was more of it showing. George was shivering violently but declined to leave his bear. He had never felt more helpless in his life. He would love to open Henry's steel door and pull him to safety, but Henry would not have understood. George would have looked like shredded wheat and drowned with him before either of them reached the back door. There are some times one can only wait to see what will happen; this was one of those times.

Henry's feet began to slide slowly down the wall; then suddenly his nose disappeared beneath the water. George's heart began pounding. Had the rescue attempt failed so soon? Ten, fourteen, twenty seconds passed and no Henry. George began to wade toward Henry's door. He had to do something. Thirty seconds, no bear. George fumbled for his keys, and while he did Henry surfaced, coughing and sputtering. In the darkness of the grotto, Henry had struggled under water to find higher ground. He had mercifully struggled in the right direction. He found the front of the cage where he could stand on his concrete drinker and hold the bars. From this position he would be able to last until the water was drained. Henry shook the water from his face, eyes, and ears, and after he did he found himself staring at George, who was smiling though teary. "Silly old bear," said George as he wiped his nose and choked back a sob.

Henry stared at George—his bear brain trying to sort out whether George was causing this calamity or fixing it. He ended up giving George a what-took-you-so-long look and moaned a little to show his discomfort.

The water was now draining noticeably, and it was clear he would live to throw another tantrum. Hundreds more, maybe thousands. He lived to a ripe old age, impressive for any bear.

How about you? Do your circumstances make you feel like you're struggling just to keep your head above water? Is it dark; and for the life of you, you can't see an end to the trial? This is the time to dig in, hang in, and wait for a chance to get to higher ground.

We are all characters in a book, and we are all in a chapter, perhaps a chapter that isn't going very well at all. I can assure you of two good things: This chapter will end for good or for evil and a better chapter will follow. The really good news is that our book has a happy ending if we know Jesus. If you're the kind that turns to the other end of the book to see how the story ends, then think on these:

"But the people who trust the Lord will become strong again" (Isa. 40:31).

"You will be sad, but your sadness will become joy" (John 16:20).

"The only temptations that you have are the temptations that all people have. But you can trust God. He will not let you be tempted more than you can stand. But when you are tempted, God will also give you a way to escape that temptation. Then you will be able to stand it" (1 Cor. 10:13).

"Even when we were with you, we told you that we all would have to suffer" (1 Thess. 3:4).

"Share in the troubles that we have. Accept them like a true soldier of Christ Jesus" (2 Tim. 2:3).

Struggling to keep your head above water? Remember, help is on the way. God may seem slow, but He is never late!

Henry the Sloth Bear was a study in courage and bad humor.

The Killer Ostrich

One of the assumptions anyone would make about animal keepers is that they love animals. It would be true most of the time but not all of the time. I met one keeper who hated animals and several who described what they did as just a job. I would describe myself as an animal lover; and after working seven years at a zoo, I think a fair statement would be, "I was able to love all of the animals some of the time, some of the animals all of the time, but I was not able to love all of the animals all of the time." Abraham Lincoln would have said that had he been a zoo-keeper.

If you're an animal lover and take the Will Rogers' position, "You never met an animal you didn't like," then I would have to assume that you never met Howard the ostrich. If you had met Howard the ostrich, you would know that animals, too, can attain an obnoxious, repulsive, gross, vain, pompous, and undesirable state of being.

There is a long-standing myth that ostriches bury their heads in the sand, thinking that they are hiding from their enemies. That isn't true at all. But after spending more than my share of time with Howard, I am willing to reopen the myth discussion and argue that ostriches do occasionally stick their heads in the sand, looking for their misplaced brains—brains that thoughtful animals, animals with good taste and manners have buried for the sake of esthetics and sanitation.

The ostrich is an animal with beautiful eyes, and, my goodness, you could hang your coat on their eyelashes. But go ahead. Look deep into their eyes for a minute and you'll discover that nobody is home. You're looking at the front door of a black hole, a vacuum so intense that it is the essence of emptiness. Don't get too close; you have to be suspicious of any animal's intellect when its eyes ride a bit higher on the skull than its brain.

Even the Holy Bible is not very complimentary of the ostrich's intelligence, making mention that she occasionally steps on her eggs and breaks them. It does say, however, that she runs like the wind. Even with the fast running part, you still don't find anything noble about the beast. Try to apply the same statement to a human mother and see how she fares. She occasionally steps on her babies, hurting them; but you ought to see her run. Somehow running fast doesn't get her off the hook. Birds ought to fly, but out of ten thousand individual species, only four were not allowed the honor. The Kiwi is cute, and I think the Lord kept it close to the ground because He wanted us to be able to see it. As for the other three, ostriches, emus and cassowaries, I think the Lord took into account their size and lack of intelligence and felt the world would be a safer place and cleaner if they were permanently grounded.

Howard was moved to my section at the zoo because he had posed too much of a danger to his keeper in the main zoo. The keeper couldn't accomplish his work because he was having to fend off Howard, all of the time.

Now for all I have said about Howard I have not said the worst—Howard was dangerous. Weighing in at over 200 pounds, he was very capable of killing a man and had spent a great deal of his energy attempting to get George Gast, his keeper. George was nerve-worn at having to beat Howard back all the time. One unguarded moment could be George's last.

I wasn't excited about being Howard's new keeper, but taking care of animals that were surplused was my job. I had a good-hearted senior keeper, Al Franklin. Al decided that until Howard the ostrich was sold, he would stand by whenever I was cleaning and feeding in Howard's yard. I felt very good about that.

When we entered the exhibit Howard would begin his mating ritual. He would drop to a crouching position and fan his wings one at a time and rock back and forth. He would become very passionate and approach us as if we were females. We, of course, were not impressed. This made Howard very angry, and that's when the aggressive behavior would begin.

Most people don't realize that the ostrich is a high risk animal. Their powerful legs can drive massive and lethal three-inch toenails deep into a rival's body. They have torn the insides from men whom they have kicked.

Al controlled Howard with a leaf rake. By placing it under his chin, he could keep him safely away from me while I cleaned the exhibit. It worked super, and days went by without incident. The bad days came when Al went on vacation and the zoo was caught shorthanded. Being a bit proud, I was reluctant to ask for help. George Gast had never asked for help and I wouldn't have either, if Al had not insisted. But Al was gone, and I must go it alone.

I had a plan. *Be aggressive,* I thought. The first day I went in alone. I took the leaf rake and ran at Howard as if I were the one doing the attacking. It took him by surprise and he ran from me. The yard we were in was nearly half an acre, and I ran him all the way to the back of it. He paced nervously when there was nowhere else to run.

"Listen, Howard, you and I will do just fine if you stay way from me when I'm here to clean and feed," I said firmly. I was then free to clean and feed the deer and pigmy goats that shared the yard with Howard.

I wondered why George Gast had had such a terrible problem with Howard. *He should have been more aggressive,* I thought. *Howard just required persistent authority.* For a week Howard kept his distance; and if he didn't, he received a hearty reminder which kept him in line.

The day came when Howard had had enough of me. I don't know what changed, what thought process, if any, brought him back to his former ways. But there Howard was at the gate, so close that it was hard to open. He was in full mating display, looking at me as if I were his female. I pushed my way in, forced the rake under his chin and yelled, "Get back. We're not going to go through this again." Howard stood and pressed against the rake. He startled me by leaping and kicking. The rake kept him at a safe distance and he began to give ground. I was feeling mastery over the beast, and pride ruled as I backed him step by step to the far reaches of the yard.

For good measure I thrust the rake at Howard in a threatening gesture. The end of the rake fell off and Howard and I stared at it in disbelief. Then both of us came to the same conclusion. *I was in real trouble!* Our eyes met and there was fire in his and fear in mine.

His eyes narrowed to malevolent slits and he was no longer a goofy-looking flightless bird. He was a dragon and I a knight, a swordless knight without armor. This dragon didn't know much, but he knew a naked knight with no weapons when he saw one—and there was no fear in his eyes. He leaped high in the air and toward me, kicking with great force. He narrowly missed me, and when he landed I could feel the ground shake. A massive dose of adrenalin surged through my system and my heart throbbed like a rapid-fire machine gun. I was experiencing the fight-or-flight syndrome and quickly chose flight. I gained about ten yards while he recovered from his leap and began to pursue me. The ostrich can run as fast as a race horse, so he began to close the gap quickly. Fifty yards away was a large metal hay manger in the middle of the yard. It was about thirty feet from the gate that led to safety. If I couldn't make it to that hay manger, that ostrich would surely kick me to death; I knew it and he knew it. I strained every muscle in my legs and leaned forward to achieve as much speed as possible.

I made it to the hay manger, grabbed it, and made a quick turn. I was on one side with Howard on the other. I was trembling violently and my legs were wobbly and weak. Our eyes met again and the ostrich focused on me. He had the look of a predator. You've seen it on your cat when it bends low and flattens its ears and stares at the sparrow on your front lawn. I was the prey and I didn't much like being looked at like that. It made me angry and afraid at the same time. "Listen, Howard," I muttered. "You had better not let me get out of this yard, because I won't be coming back alone and I'll be carrying more than a broken rake."

Howard didn't seem impressed. He just began to stalk me slowly around and around the hay manger. I kept it between him and me.

You get funny thoughts when you're in a bind like this. I started thinking, *What if I get dizzy and fall down? What if I faint?* Now those thoughts were not a comfort, and a new surge of adrenalin coursed through my system, making my heart pound harder than ever. I began to stare at the gate, wondering if it were possible to run thirty feet, pull up the latch, and shut it before Godzilla the ostrich squished me like a grape. We kept circling the hay manger. Finally, he stopped and pretended to have given up the chase. He looked away, but I knew this was displacement activity, an instinctive ploy to catch me off guard. I faked a run to the gate, and Howard was out of the chute like a rocket. "Fooled you, Howard," I taunted. "You'll have to do better than that to catch me."

We circled the manger again and Howard noticed some grain on the ground that he pecked at. I wasn't positive, but it looked like his concentration was broken, interest span taxed. The manger was between Howard and me, so now was as good a time as any to go for the gate. I pushed off the manger, knowing I had better be right. I had covered ten feet before Howard reacted, but when he did he was quick. As I was grabbing the gate, I looked back to see Howard bearing down on me at full speed. His eyes were aflame. I pulled up the hasp and backed up slightly to pull the gate open. I slipped around the gate just as Howard ran into it, knocking it shut. For good measure he jumped and kicked the fence. It wavered under the force of the blow.

Howard walked around nervously for several minutes, staring at me from time to time, daring me to come back into the exhibit. I knew Howard couldn't get away with this or no one would be safe in this yard again. I looked for and found a good friend who was a keeper and explained my need. I asked him if he would do some light cleaning while I reestablished my authority with Howard. He knew Howard and had to work with him now and then. He was glad to help. We both took shovels and rakes. I pulled on the end of mine to be sure that it would not fall off. When my friend and I stepped into the exhibit, Howard was on us like a tick on a hound. I was ready. This time I had a dirt rake and lifted it under Howard's chin and pushed. I maintained a safe distance and within a few minutes I had him moving to wherever I wanted him to be. He was administered no pain. What I was doing was necessary. There was nowhere to lock him up while caring for him. Healthy respect must be reestablished if anyone would safely care for Howard and his cage mates again.

I never went in with him again without back-up. All I had to do was ask for help for a few days until Al returned and everyone was glad to say yes, knowing they might need this kind of help also.

Howard was the worst, but difficult animals were dotted throughout the zoo.

I had cared for a Stanley Crane that was a real pain. Literally. We called him Stanley. Stanley wasn't as large as Howard but considerably more tactical. Stanley was disarming, stately, and charming, an African crane of gray elegance. He was about three-and-a-half feet tall and walked as would a duke or count. He was very territorial and didn't like any other upright animals strutting around in his exhibit. Stanley knew that he was no match for a man, so he always planned his attacks from the backside. His beak was a spear, his head a hammer. Stanley loved to let you get him completely involved in your work and then sneak up behind you and thrust his beak wickedly into your bottom. That'll wake you up, not to mention make you bleed. Stanley nailed me two times before I decided to keep one eye on him. I remember noticing Stanley sneaking up behind me so I played along with him. My peripheral vision picked him up about three feet behind me, and when he pulled his head back to thrust, I wheeled around and grabbed for his head. He injured my hand, but I grabbed him and threw him carefully into his pool where for a few sputtering moments he lost his dignity. He never bothered me after that, remembering how I had gotten the best of him.

There was never a time at the zoo when I didn't care for an animal that was difficult. It was the same for all of us. Grant Stevens cared for an African monkey that loved to sneak up on him and yank tufts of hair from his head. Dale had a dangerous eagle that dived at him in a threatening manner. Pappy Giles was knocked flat by a greater kudu that was never safe during breeding season. Casey the Guanaco, a Llama type animal, spit large globs of spit on Tom Bodie almost daily.

I'm forty-five, and when I think about it, life has always been like a zoo. In the cradle it was diaper rash. In elementary school it was bullies and teachers who had pets or couldn't teach. In high school it was unrequited love and rejection and problems at home. College was more of the same. In career it was the boss sometimes—or grasping employees. At home it has been finances or relationships. Actually, my career in the church has been most like the zoo. Occasionally there have been killer sheep in the flocks (present flock excepted) that were far more dangerous than Howard.

Jesus warned us that in this world we would have tribulation, but we really don't want to believe Him. He has told us that it is given to our brotherhood to suffer, but we don't want to hear that either.

The bottom line is that the world is full of Stanleys and Howards, bullies and bad teachers, bosses and killer sheep. Life is often a walk through the valley, and it is there and only there that our character is made strong and deep.

But if you belong to Jesus, He has made wonderful promises that He will keep for He cannot lie. This is one of them.

"It is the same with you. Now you are sad. But I will see you again and you will be happy. And no one will take away your joy" (John 16:22).

The Ostrich is surprisingly one of the zoo's more dangerous animals with which to work.

Ladybug

When I was seven our family obtained a small black and tan puppy and named her Ladybug. I do not recall where we got her, but even after twenty-five years have come and gone I can vividly recall the warmth of her head lying across my bare feet or the look of love in her eyes as she watched to see if she would be invited on any adventure that led her beyond the boundaries of our yard. She was an ardent traveler and loved to ride in the car. No dog ever born enjoyed more the wind whipping her ears and flapping her lips as she leaned as far as we would permit out the back window of our '53 Chevrolet station wagon.

She weighed in at about fifteen pounds, maybe twenty, and the consensus was that she was a cross between a cocker spaniel and a beagle.

Ladybug was a happy dog and ticklish. If you scratched her in just the right place she actually smiled.

Now I know that's hard to believe, but, hang it all, she smiled, and if you saw it you would call it that too.

When I was young I actually thought of her as a member of the family. She was the youngest child. To me she was Ladybug Richmond. She slept with us, and many was the morning that I was licked awake. Between the ages of seven and nine I never washed my ears because Ladybug did it for me almost every morning.

She did have a fault that remained with her all the days of her life. She had breath that you could see on a warm day. Whatever doggy breath is, she had twice as much as should be allotted. We had to apologize for it more than once. She was also possessed of a great capacity for natural gas production and could not contain it.

Ladybug was my friend and shadow, and I always loved her but never more than the one summer day that I asked for and obtained her forgiveness. Here is what happened.

I was raised in Altadena, California, a small friendly town nestled against the San Gabriel Mountains. You have seen these very mountains if you have watched the Rose Parade or the Rose Bowl Game. The San Gabriels watch over Pasadena and Altadena and most of the Los Angeles basin. Now Altadena had much to commend it, but right up there at the top, smack dab in the middle of the "amen corner" was Kern's Delicatessen. Old Mr. Kern had located some of the finest culinary delights known to the palates of our species. His Swiss cheese, pumpernickel bread, and kosher dill pickles were the best. It was a four-block walk to the deli, but I would make the walk anytime some benefactor would finance the pilgrimage.

One very hot summer afternoon in deep August I had a little extra cash and remembered how much I enjoyed biting into one of Mr. Kern's renowned kosher dills. I was with a friend, Doug Sigler, and asked if he would like to walk to Kern's with me. As it turned out, my brother and a friend of his decided to go also. When we got to the front door, Ladybug was wiggling with delight for she was sure we were going to let her come along. After a little banter, we agreed and were out the door on our way to the gates of heaven.

Ladybug was not leashed because she would never bite anyone. She was always bounding just ahead, stopping now and then to smell something and make a memory. She would run over and jump on us now and then to let us know she was glad to be part of the adventure. Ladybug was five going on six at the time, and I was going into the seventh grade in the fall.

When we arrived at Kern's, I purchased one piece of his pumpernickel bread, one slice of aged Swiss cheese, one large kosher dill pickle, and a bottle of Dad's Old Fashioned Root Beer. We had told Ladybug to sit at the front door and wait for us while we ate inside. Life doesn't get better than eating at Kern's Delicatessen with family and friends. We left only after licking our fingers clean, for leaving anything uneaten would have been a sin.

Once outside we ordered Ladybug to follow us home. Twenty steps down the street we looked into the Hillcrest Pharmacy window and noticed the latest issue of *Mad Magazine.* We again ordered Ladybug to sit on the sidewalk and wait for us while we went in the store. We all read *Mad Magazine* over my friend's shoulder and laughed at the absurd humor of the latest issue. Laughter's tears streamed down our faces. The store clerk asked us to buy or fly, so we left. We left a little embarrassed and a little miffed. We also left through the back door, which provided a shortcut home. We left Ladybug waiting patiently at the front door of Hillcrest Pharmacy.

On the way home we groused over being given the bum's rush. The afternoon began to blend with evening, and our friends both left for home and dinner. My dad came home from a hard day's work in construction and, after washing up, called us to the dinner table. It was a meat and potatoes meal and had a lot of the kind of leftovers any family dog would kill for. My father scraped them onto a plate and stepped out the back door to call for Ladybug.

She didn't come. He asked Steve and me if we had seen her, and we both looked at each other. I didn't know for sure what Steve was going to do, but I was trying to figure out a way to blame our thoughtless mistake on him. I refused to answer, hoping that if my brother spoke first he would get most of the blame for losing our dog. Steve finally admitted that we had left her outside the pharmacy. My Dad had a disgusted look, which he administered pretty equally as I remember. He told us to jump in the car, and we backed out of our driveway a lot faster than usual. He didn't say much, but he did inquire if we had traded our brains for sawdust. We knew well that we better not answer that particular question. If we said no, we were smart-mouthing. If we said yes, we were smart-mouthing. So we both did what he wanted us to do; we looked guilty and stupid and kept quiet. Now I don't know what you're thinking, but I don't agree with the notion that there are no appropriate times for a tongue-lashing. God did it all the time to Israel, and Jesus did it to His disciples. Steve and I were getting less than we deserved, and I knew it even then.

My father knew enough about dogs to know that Ladybug was capable of following her own scent home, so he followed the route we had walked to the delicatessen. The farther we drove without seeing her the worse I felt. I had let down one of my best friends and I knew it. I had a lump in my throat as I began to picture my dog run over by a car or cringing in the back of a cage at the dog pound. We finally rounded the corner of Mariposa Lane and Lake Street and saw a small dark form curled into a ball by the front door of the pharmacy. Steve stuck his head out the window and yelled, "Here, girl."

His yell awoke her, and she bounced against the glass thinking we were still in the store. Steve left the car and picked her up.

I have never witnessed a more emotional reunion. Ladybug wiggled until I thought she would fall apart. She whined happily all the way home and licked every hand that came within a foot of her.

My father, happy about the outcome, said, "All's well that ends well, but don't you to ever let that happen to your dog again. I don't have to tell you all the bad things that could have happened to her, do I?" We nodded.

That night I asked Ladybug if she wanted to sleep with me. Her tail wagged as she ran ahead of me and jumped up on the bed. When I turned out the light, I called her to come close and I hugged her and told her how sorry I was to have let her down. She just kissed me and rolled over to have me scratch her tummy. I did that until we both fell asleep.

Ladybug was always anxious to forgive. Her only desire was that she be part of a family, our family, her family. The saying that dogs are man's best friends really isn't so far off in my experience.

You know what made me remember this story? I was reading the story of the prodigal son in the fifteenth chapter of Luke. It is my favorite story in the Bible. As I thought about the father in the story, I was impressed by how anxious he was to forgive and be reunited to his son. The story answers the question, "How does God feel when we are off blowing it?" He is simply longing and waiting for us to come to our senses and come home. He is always, as my dog was with my brother and me, glad for the reunion. If you have been away from God for awhile and want to know how He feels, read this. If you want to know what to do about it, follow the prodigal son's lead and come home just as he did. Read it for yourself.

> Then Jesus said, "A man had two sons. The younger son said to his father, 'Give me my share of the property.' So the father divided the property between his two sons. Then

the younger son gathered up all that was his and left. He traveled far away to another country. There he wasted his money in foolish living. He spent everything that he had. Soon after that, the land became very dry, and there was no rain. There was not enough food to eat anywhere in the country. The son was hungry and needed money. So he got a job with one of the citizens there. The man sent the son into the fields to feed pigs. The son was so hungry that he was willing to eat the food the pigs were eating. But no one gave him anything. The son realized that he had been very foolish. He thought, 'All of my father's servants have plenty of food. But I am here, almost dying with hunger. I will leave and return to my father. I'll say to him: Father, I have sinned against God and have done wrong to you. I am not good enough to be called your son. But let me be like one of your servants.' So the son left and went to his father.

"While the son was still a long way off, his father saw him coming. He felt sorry for his son. So the father ran to him, and hugged and kissed him. The son said, 'Father, I have sinned against God and have done wrong to you. I am not good enough to be called your son.' But the father said to his servants, 'Hurry! Bring the best clothes and put them on him. Also, put a ring on his finger and sandals on his feet. And get our fat calf and kill it. Then we can have a feast and celebrate! My son was dead, but now he is alive again! He was lost, but now he is found!' So they began to celebrate."

Luke 15:11–24

Mosquitoes and Flies

It is both comforting and disturbing to know that God has created everything for a specific purpose. Nothing was an accident; nothing was unplanned. Not one of the 4.4 million creatures that fly, walk, swim, crawl, wriggle, slide, or hop the earth was a joke or an afterthought. Everything does something that makes its own existence worthwhile. Each thing performs a foreordained function that benefits nature and glorifies God.

In Ecclesiates 3:14 we read, "I know anything God does will continue forever. People cannot add anything to what God has done. And they cannot take anything away from it." When God created the earth and all of the animals, it was complete. Moreover, He said that everything was good. But many Christians I have met don't share that view. They want to apologize for some of God's most amazing inventions—His animals. Even worse, they take delight in stepping on them, shooting them, running over them, and swatting them until each amazing spark of life is extinguished.

I am referring to a host of vermin that man finds repulsive: spiders, snakes, roaches, rats, and mosquitoes and flies, to name a few. The average middle-class Christian is quietly embarrassed about these creations and would gladly let the devil take credit for them if they could. Well, it's time that someone took up their defense and made sure that God received the glory for the great things that He has done. I mean to include all the aforementioned creatures in my defense. On the day that God made them He declared that they were good. The Scriptures make clear that what God has declared to be good we have no business declaring evil.

Perhaps we fear these creatures because we tend to fear what we least understand. The creature that we most understand is man, so when we see creatures that do not remind us of our species we are repulsed. We are afraid of snakes and spiders because they do not look like man. Snakes don't have enough arms and legs to remind us of men, and spiders have too many. On the other hand, we are attracted to species that do resemble man.

Go to your local Hallmark store and make a note of what animals you see on greeting cards. You will find primates first (monkeys and apes) and then bears. Psychologists have known this for years, and the greeting-card companies have taken advantage of psychological studies to make a profit. Other than butterflies, when have you seen resting on the rack a greeting card with an insect or spider? If you do, it's sure to be a cartoon that has been made to look like a caricature of a human. Check this out for yourself next time you're at the store.

Fear is the basis of our revulsion. And we hate what we fear.

On many occasions I have asked the question, "Why do you think God made mosquitoes and flies?" The answer is usually very self-centered. People, even the educated, say it was to punish and harass sinful man. It has rarely occurred to anyone that these two amazing creatures do us far more good than harm. "No!" you say? "Yes!" I answer emphatically. "How?" you respond. I'm so glad you asked. Let me tell you how in a story—not a fiction exactly but a fiction based entirely on fact. In fact this story is unfolding somewhere on the earth as it is written and again as you are reading it.

Tonda the white-tailed deer stood proudly in the afternoon sun and watched over the small herd of females that followed him from feeding ground to feeding ground. His species was browsers. This means that they ate leaves. It was spring now, and the trees at the base of the mountain were beginning to bud, forming new leaves soft and sweet. The herd was glad, for they were tired of the dry leaves they had survived on during the winter.

The leaves were forming in the valley where Tonda led his herd but not in the mountains where the snow was just now beginning to melt. The spring rains had formed pools and ponds in the lower valleys, and the warming trend had awakened the insects that had slept all winter.

Diptera, a female mosquito, had mated with a chance male and eggs had begun to form inside her. Her instincts told her she must have blood or her young would not be strong and healthy. The nectar that her species normally drinks is low in the protein necessary to form her eggs. So she, along with thousands of her kind, began to seek out animals that they could pierce in order to obtain the blood that the young needed to survive. Only the females of her kind bite anyone and only then for the good of their young.

As the sun was setting, Diptera found Tonda and settled near his eye. She landed so softly Tonda had no idea that he was being visited. She pierced his flesh and injected a small amount of saliva. The saliva created an irritation that caused swelling, signaling the body to send more blood to repair the area. She was bloating on blood even before Tonda began to itch. He rubbed his nose against the lower branch of the black oak whose tender young leaves he was devouring with relish. Diptera flew just before she would have been crushed by the movement.

She flew until she smelled water and landed at the edge of a small pound. She lowered her abdomen into the pond and laid several dozen eggs. When she finished, she flew to feed on the nectar she would find at the center of the tiny flowers beginning to herald spring.

Diptera was the first to bite Tonda that night but not the last. He was bitten fifty times as the other expectant mothers sought out protein for their young. Tonda knew instinctively that it was time to climb the mountain. The higher he would go the fewer the mosquitoes. So he began to walk up the hillside until the night air had just a bit of a bite to it. Here the mosquitoes would continue to sleep for five or six more days. Tonda browsed again, free of the annoying mosquitoes' bites.

In the valley Diptera wriggled deep into the bloom of a small purple flower and sipped a bit of nectar. As she sipped, a bit of pollen stuck to her body. It rubbed off in the next bloom, giving the next plant the power to make seeds. Diptera and her species actually pollinate as many flowers as bees but are rarely given credit for their efforts.

Tonda discovered seven days later that the mosquitoes were again at work. So he moved up again. As he moved, the herd pruned the lower branches of the trees on which they fed, allowing light to penetrate to the new growth of grasses and plants near the base of the trees. The herd fertilized as they went. Now spring was moving them higher and higher to be relieved of the insatiable appetite of the mosquitoes.

By late spring the snows were all but melted, and the deer had reached the highest elevation. Millions of mosquitoes clambered for blood as summer set in. They fought to reach small pools and ponds, and even at ten thousand feet the deer were harassed by the tiny marauders. Tonda's instincts told him that they needed to return to lower elevations where the pools had now dried up. There they would again find relief—at least the numbers would be significantly less.

In the valley below Diptera was again heading for a small lake where she could deposit her eggs. A violet-green swallow hunting for small insects saw her, swooped down, and in a second captured the mosquito. She was fed to the swallow's young that evening, and even the small drop of blood she had extracted from a rabbit was not wasted. The young swallow enjoyed it immensely as his mother filled his crop.

Summer gave way to fall. Now Tonda and his herd again felt the bite of cooler nights and the boredom of falling leaves. The moderate climate of the valley again beckoned them, so down they came.

Late one afternoon the herd was surprised by a mountain lion. The does and now older fawns ran for their lives, but Tonda with his awesome rack of antlers stayed to fight. Because of a powerful hunger, the mountain lion decided to brave the powerful buck. Tonda held his ground while the cat looked for an opening. As it charged, Tonda lowered his head and drove his antlers deep into the predator's chest. It turned out to be a fatal encounter for the mountain lion, but before it died it sank its fangs deep into the shoulder of the brave stag.

Tonda stood panting over the dead cat and felt the stabbing pain from the wound in his shoulder. He turned and limped his way down the hill to join his herd once again.

In the morning Tonda was awakened by the buzzing of flies around the wound. Many had dined on the dried blood and had recognized that the wound would be an excellent place to lay their eggs. The eggs soon hatched, and their larvae (maggots) began to eat the dead and decaying flesh in and around the wound. God has made the maggots to eat only dead and decaying flesh. Consequently the new growth was kept free from infection, and the two-inch wound was allowed to heal from the inside out. Had the flies never found Tonda, he would surely have died, for the bite of any cat is very nasty and apt to infect.

This wasn't the first time flies had saved his life. When he was a young buck, he had fought for and lost the right to run with the females. He had had four deep wounds from Dovar the mighty buck. The flies had come at that time too and cleaned his wounds, allowing him to live. Flies clean all dead and decaying things. They consume and eliminate, and the plants absorb their waste for food. The flies live but six weeks and are themselves food for many animals. Those not eaten by animals leave their bodies to the earth for plant food. The healthy plants take in what we breathe out and give us oxygen in return.

So it was that Tonda returned to the valley, having served the forest while ascending and descending the mountain. The mosquito was his herdsman and the fly his doctor. The mosquito also helped the plants to seed, and the fly helped the plants to feed.

Made to harass man you say? I hope you do not say so anymore. Up until 1932 maggots were still being used by human doctors to do the same things for humans that they still do for deer. There are few humans alive whose ancestors were not saved by maggots after having been bitten by a beast or pierced by a sword. Guess what? If you are badly burned, your doctor will still probably ask you to allow him to introduce maggots to your wounds. They will remove the dead tissue more skillfully than could any human surgeon.

Do you still want to give Satan credit for mosquitoes and flies? He couldn't even make gnats.

Practical Jokes

I'm not sure when it all began, but I have been a practical joker for a long time. I can't remember ever having played a joke which actually hurt anyone physically or wounded them emotionally, though I did once play one I wish I could take back. I have played plenty of the kind that scare people witless for a second or two or put someone on the spot. My jokes are generally reserved for good friends, which may have inspired the saying, "With friends like you who needs enemies?"

My first attempts at practical joking occurred when I was six years old. At that time I liked to entertain myself by hiding in my grandparents' closets at bedtime. When they would come for their night clothes, I would leap out at them and yell, "Yaaaah." It normally caught their attention, and I noticed that my grandfather would reach for his heart if I was particularly effective. I remember my father saying, "Gary, your grandfather has a very weak heart, and when you scare him like that, you could make it stop. So I want you to stop scaring Grandpa or Grandma. If you don't, I'm going to spank your bottom shiny red." And he would have, too, but I stopped and there was no need.

When I was eight I took up the habit again, only my brother became the victim of my terrible desire to scare people. He was twelve, and his bedtime was thirty minutes later than mine. We shared the same room. I always had thirty wonderful minutes in which to conceive a plan, and I must admit that the anticipation of a joke is often much more satisfying than the joke itself.

Sometimes I put pillows under the covers to make it look as if I was asleep when he came in, but I would be in the closet ready to leap out. Sometimes I would hide behind the door and grab him going by. Sometimes I would hide under his bed and grab his arm when it would dangle towards the floor. My favorite was when he would pull back my covers to see if I was really there and I would be. Then I would rise up and yell "Raaaah" with my eyes wide open and an ugly expression on my face.

Though my brother was four years older, I was able to generate an enormous volume of insecurity, so much so that he was afraid to come to bed. Our walls were thin, and I remember hearing my brother beg my father to come in and check where I was and if I was really asleep. My father would say, "For goodness sake, Steve, what's wrong with you? You're twelve years old, and your little brother's only eight. Get in there and get to bed!" A couple of times my father did, at my brother's request, come in and check. But I was always pretending to be asleep when he did. My brother has never really forgotten those wonderful days. He still wonders what awful sin he had committed at an early age to deserve me as his little brother.

When I was twelve I began to graduate from simple scare jokes to jokes that took some thought. It was also the year that I played the only joke I truly regret. It was one of those it-seemed-like-a-good-idea-at-the-time kind of jokes born of an idle mind. You know what they say: "An idle mind is the devil's playground."

The Devil's Playground

I don't know about you, but, left with too much idle time, I am likely to become a public nuisance. It has always been that way for me. When I was young my father impressed me with pithy sayings. One of his favorites was "An idle mind is the devil's playground." That saying applied to me would be better stated, "Gary's idle mind is the devil's national park."

When I was in the seventh grade, I was given the opportunity to join the school orchestra. I really wasn't the orchestra type, but the alternate class had homework to which I was allergic. So I turned in my textbook and followed Mr. Palmer, the aging orchestra director, to the band room where he invited his new recruits to try the different instruments found in the orchestra. The violin seemed too feminine. The cello held no appeal, because I knew the boy I would be sitting next to and had no desire to catch cooties. (It was a well-known fact that he had had them for a long time.) The closet door was open, and there stood a string bass. It was love at first sight. When first I plucked the massive strings, I could feel the resonance rumble through my body. This was a man's instrument. I would be a bassist.

In no time Mr. Palmer had an eager crop of seventh graders pulling bows across strings and blowing enthusiastically into wood, chrome, and brass. The sound resembled what might be produced by a group of children jumping up and down on cats and parrots. When I was young I thought of Mr. Palmer as a dedicated teacher and lover of fine music, but as I look back now I wonder what dark sin he was attempting to atone for by locking himself in a room five hours a day with junior-high musicians.

Orchestra was not always fun and games—no, not by a long shot. With twenty-one new students, Mr. Palmer's time was very limited. We did more waiting than playing on most days, while he gave each student individual instruction. We were also told to stand or sit quietly while he worked with the other students. I don't know what my problem was, but I had an all-consuming desire to fill silent moments with sound. Sometimes I talked, sometimes I plucked, and occasionally I belched.

Mr. Palmer appeared to be a patient man, but there were those glances at the clock. (I think he was waiting for the retirement bell to ring.) In spite of his patience, he did have a line. And when you crossed it, as I did on several occasions, he had a fiendishly effective punishment. I have since wondered why our own prison system has not employed it for the rehabilitation of the more hardened criminal.

When I crossed the line, I would be sent to his office. And I can speak with firsthand knowledge that there is no greater state of boredom than when left alone for thirty minutes or more in a band director's office. There were band magazines (all printed in black and white). You could go through years of them and never be sure you were not looking at the same one over and over again. I knew in my heart that a picture of Elvis or Fats Domino would never brighten this room, this desolate closet of mediocrity.

One day, again banished to boredom, I found myself looking from place to place to see if anything new had fallen or had been left behind. Perhaps a kindred spirit had hidden a note or something in an attempt to make contact with a fellow inmate. I glanced under Mr. Palmer's desk, but all I saw were his marching shoes. They were old, cracked by the moisture they had absorbed from years of marching the band over the morning dew on the school football field. The toes were curled up, and most of the shoe dye had faded.

As I looked up, my eyes focused on the wall-mounted pencil sharpener. It was full to the brim with pencil shavings. Something to do, I thought. I will be helpful. I removed the sharpener's shaving chamber and reached under the desk to dump the contents into the wastebasket. As I did, my attention was drawn again to the rustic marching shoes. I looked at the shoes . . . then the shavings . . . then the shoes. I had found a better place to dump the shavings. I poured half the contents into each shoe, then carefully lifted each shoe into my lap and packed the shavings firmly into the toe area until I had clearly reduced the size by at least an inch. I replaced the shoes to their place under the desk and giggled. I theorized that this had probably been the coolest event that had ever occurred in this office. I left school that day, wishing I could be there when Mr. Palmer tried to put on his shoes and discovered they were far too tight. Having a healthy imagination, I was able to enjoy the thought of it as much as if I were actually there to experience it firsthand. The more I thought about it, the funnier it became. I actually laughed out loud on several occasions during the rest of the day.

It was about a week later when I was to discover just how my joke had gone. As I was walking out the door, Mr. Palmer grasped my shoulder rather firmly and asked if he might talk to me for just a second. I agreed and knew in an instant what we would most likely be talking about.

"Gary, Gary, Gary," he began. "You're not in trouble, but I really must know if my suspicions are correct. Last Friday when I practiced with the band, I put on my marching shoes. They are like old friends to me, you see, and fit perfectly—at least they had until last Friday. That day the toes seemed awfully full." He squeezed my shoulder harder, and just for a second I had the illusion that he was going for my neck. He continued, "When I removed my shoes my heart sank. You see, my wife had given me a special pair of socks made of white Angora wool for my birthday. I have a touch of arthritis and varicose veins, and these socks provided a feeling of warmth and support that makes marching less painful. Those socks are now white with dark gray toes. The dark gray won't wash out, bleach out, or come out with any cleaning fluid known to man. Gary, those socks cost my wife $7.00 (this was in 1956), and she's got fire in her eyes. I'm not going to tell anybody if I find out who put the shavings in my shoes; but, Gary, were you the one?"

He looked so hurt as he stared deep into my eyes. I wasn't always good, but I wasn't a liar at heart either, so I hung my head and said, "Yes, Mr. Palmer, I did it. I'm very sorry. I didn't know I would do so much damage. May I please get you a new pair of socks?"

"No, Gary, I couldn't let you do that. But whatever you do, don't let my wife know that it was you—not if you want to make it to the eighth grade."

Mr. Palmer gave my shoulder a final squeeze, a sort of "you're forgiven" squeeze and walked into his office. He sat down slowly and leaned on his desk. I'm not sure, but I sometimes wonder if that was one of the many days he had asked himself the question "Is teaching worth it?"

I felt terrible. Here was a man who had been nice to me in every way, and during a thoughtless moment, an idle moment, I used my time to hurt him and his wife.

I think idle time is when energy is available, nothing is planned, and we use our energy for destructive purposes. During idle time I am most likely to gossip, be critical, be frivolous, and, maybe worst of all, worry. During idle time I am most likely to wallow in self-pity, watch too much television, envy another's success, or enjoy their defeat.

Time is the one thing that comes equally to the rich and to the poor, and all will have to give an account of how they used it. One man wisely said, "No man left his footprints on the sands of time sitting on his duff. And who wants to leave their duff prints on the sands of time?"

The Bible speaks clearly on time: "So be very careful how you live. Do not live like those who are not wise. Live wisely. I mean that you should use every chance you have for doing good, because these are evil times" (Eph. 5:15–16).

Today is the best day of all to ask, "What are we doing with the time God has given us? It's all we really have."

What If?

The zoo was a great place to advance an illustrious career of joking. One of my favorite zoo jokes was inspired while playing the What If? game.

I have played the What If? game since childhood. You have too, I'll bet. The really great players are blessed or cursed with active imaginations. In a group of people, what-ifers are sure to be the ones who create the most enthusiasm or inspire the most fear. I began developing my skills when I was very young, and by the fifth grade I was quite capable of what-ifing with the best of them. I am fully convinced that I was already what-ifing at high-school level, maybe higher.

I remember a conversation with my good friend, Douglas Sigler. He was also in the fifth grade and a pretty fair what-ifer himself. I said, "Doug, what if there is a bigfoot creature that lives in Eaton Canyon?" I had just heard that there might be a bigfoot type of creature in the western states, and Eaton Canyon was my favorite place in the whole world to go hiking. It was just one mile from our home in Altadena, California.

Doug looked at me as if I were a little crazy and answered, "You don't believe that junk, do you?"

"Well, there could be creatures we haven't discovered yet."

"I think we would have found one by now," Doug moaned. He rolled his eyes and gave me that "Oh, brother" look.

I felt a need to redeem myself, so I went into action. "What if these bigfoot creatures are shy but very intelligent? They could hide from people for a long time and not be found. What if they are stranded space creatures and they can make themselves invisible? They might be waiting for another spaceship to come and pick them up. Maybe the food they eat is getting harder to find, so they spend more time outside, and that's why they are getting seen more often. You can't tell me that it's not possible, 'cause everything is possible."

Doug was a little overwhelmed by my intensity, so he sat there quietly for a moment and then smiled a knowing smile. "I have an idea," said Doug. "Let's go up to Eaton Canyon and look for footprints."

"Are you kidding?" I countered. "What if those bigfoot things eat kids?"

"Are you chicken or something?" he taunted.

"No! I just think we ought to be really careful. I think we better take a weapon with us."

"A weapon?"

"Like a club or a spear or something like that."

"Oh, brother!"

Doug and I took that hike to Eaton Canyon. I had always enjoyed the canyon before. It was beautiful. A small stream snaked its way through a predetermined path at the base of granite cliffs where it had been for thousands of years. It fell over rocks and gurgled with pleasure as it played with the rays of the morning sun. I had been there dozens of times before and had always noticed those kinds of little beautiful moments, but not any longer. I was sure that bigfoot was going to jump out at me from around the next bend of the river. Doug was even getting a little jumpy.

We were terrified seconds later. A large black and brown hairy creature bounded around the corner and stopped five feet in front of us, surprised by our screaming. The biggest German shepherd I had ever seen cocked its head, wagged its tail, and ran past us. Its owner, a high-school girl, came around the bend moments later. She smiled at us as she continued her walk, but I noticed a fleeting puzzled look. I think she must have wondered why we looked so terrified.

Doug said, "If there was a bigfoot up higher, it would have gotten that girl. She was really pretty."

"Are you kidding? Didn't you see her dog? No bigfoot in its right mind would try to capture her. I'll bet that dog would die for her."

"I think you might be right. I don't think any girls are worth dying for, but she came pretty close. She was really pretty."

"I'm tired of footprint hunting. There aren't any bigfoot creatures in this part of California anyway."

"Probably not," Doug agreed.

For the life of me, I cannot remember why we kept looking over our shoulders as we left the canyon. But we did.

What-ifing carries with it an awesome power. It is the power of suggestion. The power does not diminish as one gets older. It increases.

By the time I had reached my twenty-fifth year of life, I had turned what-ifing into a science. If there were an Olympics for what-ifers, I would have been in the decathlon and it would have been held at the Los Angeles Zoo. That's where the best what-ifers trained. If you would like to observe them in training, visit the zoo at breaktime. They will what-if like crazy for twenty minutes out of every fifteen minutes of breaktime.

I remember a day in the summer of 1968 that a group of veteran keepers got together for what may have been the finest single session of what-ifing in the history of man. (No exaggeration, really.) It was very warm for ten o'clock in the morning, and the air was crystal clear, which was odd for Los Angeles. The heat brought in more keepers than usual, thinking a Coke might just hit the spot. We gathered at the North American snack bar and filled the cement picnic tables that circled the building. We enjoyed the shade and the fraternity.

It didn't take long for the conversation to turn into a what-ifing session. Don got us started. "Did you hear that some hermit has been sneaking into the zoo at night, crawling into exhibits and stealing food from the animals? Guy's nuts, I bet. What if a guy like that got ahold of a set of keys? He could let a lot of animals out in a short amount of time."

Dale added, "What if a guy like that got into the reptile house? Can you imagine what Griffith Park would be like with cobras and mambas and all sorts of vipers? You couldn't get anybody to come to the zoo for years. There'd be a big lawsuit if anybody got bit. You can count on that."

"What if that guy let Bosco the cape buffalo out? Cape buffaloes have knocked boxcars off of train tracks in Africa. I'd hate to come into the zoo some morning and find Bosco looking at me. He charges the fence now. Can you imagine what fun he'd have really knocking people around like beach balls? Did you ever watch him stand behind his fence and go into a rage? He trembles and salivates, moans and groans, and then he charges. I swear someday he won't have to wait to be let out. He's going to knock his fence down or come through the side of the barn. That Bosco is something all right."

John decided it was his moment and spoke. "Ivan's the one that gives me nightmares. What if some nutball let him out?" Everybody got real quiet because John had just mentioned the most feared animal at the zoo, a male polar bear. He seized the opportunity to run with the moment he had created.

"I was here the day Ivan killed Nanatchka. She was a pretty bear. Ivan went right after her. That's just what he'd do to us you know." John paused again for effect. Everybody was silent as they nursed their own private nightmare with Ivan. John added, "Bears don't kill you right off."

All the keepers but one left breaktime glad that they didn't have to care for Ivan. I was that one, Ivan's keeper. John's what-if seemed even more frightening because only days before one of the Kodiak bears had lifted his guillotine door and let all the other Kodiak bears out on exhibit, just seconds after the keeper had finished cleaning. The keeper would have been dead for sure if that bear had made his move any sooner. I wondered if Ivan could ever figure out how to open the door and let himself out.

I discovered on the way back from break that Jim, a relief keeper, had been assigned to help me with my string. I had been busy acid washing the elephant seal pool and was sadly behind. Ivan's exhibit had not been cleaned and neither had the penguins and pelicans on exhibit.

"Al Franklin asked me to clean Ivan's exhibit for you. He said you were behind because of acid washing. I know the routine so you don't have to show me anything."

"Thanks, Jim. I owe you one."

"Don't mention it."

Jim headed for the polar bear moat, and I went to the pelagic bird exhibit. I remembered that Jim had looked very impressed by John's dissertation, and it gave me an idea. Did I mention anywhere that keepers are incurable practical jokers? Well, they are, and they specialize in scare jokes. I knew the cleaning routine for the polar bear moat backwards and forwards. I had performed it hundreds of times myself. Jim would just now be opening up the back door to the moat. He would prop that door open to ventilate the area and walk forward five steps to unlock a sliding door. He would pull it open and slide it shut behind him. Then he would turn and look at Ivan, who was already looking at him. He would be impressed by the size of Ivan's massive paws. Ivan weighed 950 pounds and stood nearly ten feet tall. He was 100 percent nightmare and never missed a chance to swipe at a keeper. Ivan was above all things a killer. Jim would lock the guillotine door handle into place so that no one could let Ivan out on him.

Then he would open three more chain link doors that would give him access to the outdoor exhibit. Ivan's pool was already drained, so Jim would grab the one-inch hose, put on the high pressure nozzle, and turn on the water. The surge of pressure would jar his arm, and the noise inside the grotto would be deafening. He would then drag the hose down the dimly lit hallway and pull it out into the morning sun to begin cleaning the exhibit.

I timed it so that I was silently entering the back door just as Jim was beginning to clean. I stopped at the hose bib long enough to turn the hose on and off. It makes the guy outside think his hose is kinked, and he will give it a dynamic tug to relieve the problem. After doing that a couple of times, I proceeded to stalk my prey down the dimly lit hallway. All I had to do was follow the hose. As I crept up behind him I could see that he was completely involved with his task. This was going to be too easy. I stepped to within reach of my prey and let out a mighty roar. Now polar bears don't roar, but even the finest keeper would have forgotten that fact under the circumstances. I simultaneously grabbed his shoulder and side. I had never, before that day, seen anybody try to climb a high-pressure hose. I'll have to give Jim credit for one thing: he never let go of the hose through all the animation that he achieved. Boy, was he angry. People sometimes get that way when you cause them to abandon their dignity. Jim was a soft-spoken man, but he said some words with his eyes that I had never heard before or since.

Jim had been set up by the negative power of suggestion. What-ifing had taken its toll. Because we are fallen creatures, we are prone to think negatively. Our what-ifing mechanisms turned inward usually create apprehension and fear. We become victims of our own thought patterns. If we allow that to happen, we become cowards, too afraid to make a move, any move, for fear we might fail. Our imaginations have the potential to extend our faith or destroy it.

What-ifing prevented two million people from entering the Promised Land. Joshua and Caleb believed God, but everyone else forgot that the Lord would fight for them. Their imaginations took over.

Joshua described the effect of the what-ifers in Deuteronomy 1:28–33.

> Where can we go now? The spies we sent have made us afraid. They said, "The people there are bigger and taller than we are. The cities are big. They have walls up to the sky. And we saw the Anakites there!"
>
> Then I said to you, "Don't be frightened. Don't be afraid of those people. The Lord your God will go ahead of you. He will fight for you as he did in Egypt. You saw him do it. And in the desert you saw how the Lord your God carried you. He was like a man carrying his son. And he has brought you safely all the way to this place."
>
> But you still did not trust the Lord your God. As you moved, he went before you. He found places for you to camp. He went before you in a fire at night and in a cloud during the day. He showed you which way to go.

We have heard it said, "A coward dies a thousand deaths, a brave man just one."

Romans 12:2 tells us "Do not change yourselves to be like the people of this world. But be changed within by a new way of thinking. Then you will be able to decide what God wants for you. And you will be able to know what is good and pleasing to God and what is perfect."

We must change our way of thinking so that it conforms to God's will.

Negative: What if I share my faith in Christ with that person, and she thinks I'm a fruitcake or a religious nut?

Positive: What if I share my faith with that person? Maybe she will come to know Him and find peace, joy, and salvation.

Negative: What if I say no? Maybe he'll think I'm a prude. Maybe he won't ask me out anymore.

Positive: What if I said yes? I'd lose my self-respect. If he doesn't ask me out, God will provide better.

What-ifing in its negative context is nothing more than worry. And we are commanded not to worry. "Do not worry about anything. But pray and ask God for everything you need. And when you pray, always give thanks. And God's peace will keep your hearts and minds in Christ Jesus. The peace that God gives is so great that we cannot understand it" (Phil. 4:6–7).

How do we change if we are worriers (and I am)? It's a matter of forcing ourselves into new ways of thinking. Philippians 4:8 gives us the formula: "Brothers, continue to think about the things that are good and worthy of praise. Think about the things that are true and honorable and right and pure and beautiful and respected."

"But Lord, what if I can't?"

"No excuses, My child! I will be with you."

I wasn't the only one to play practical jokes at the zoo. I wasn't even the best at it. One of my favorites happened at the health center.

Jordan Johnson was one my favorite keepers. You couldn't help but like him. He was a nice guy in the tradition of Hoss Cartwright. Jordan weighed about 260 pounds and was six feet, four inches tall. I'm glad to report that I never saw him angry. He was even-tempered, the same day in and day out. He was also very gullible. Now when you combine the characteristics nice and gullible in the same person, you have to a practical joker what a bull's eye is to an archer, the best part of the target. Jordan was frequently the target for practical jokes. But even when they were dramatic, humiliating, or frightening, he would just say, "Oh, you guys." Then he'd laugh like the joke was played on someone else. Jordan was a neat guy.

One day Jordan dropped by the health center right after an unsuccessful surgery on an American black bear. The bear had just died in its cage following surgery, and in all fairness the position that it died in was very natural, as though the bear were sleeping.

Jordan looked at the bear for a while and then greeted us with, "What's happening? How's the bear doing?"

Now some of the five guys present thought the bear looked dead and realized that Jordan didn't. The principal keeper, Ken Kirk, said, "Jordan, do you have a few minutes? We're all bushed from this bear thing, and we want to get a little lunch. We'd be back in about thirty minutes if you could see your way clear to watch the bear for a while until he wakes up from the tranquilizer. What we need you to do is to count respirations per minute for us. They are between eighteen and twenty per minute right now, and that's good, but if it falls down to say nine or ten that wouldn't be good. You understand? Let me show you how to count. You take your watch off and hold it in front of your face and count how many times the bear breathes in ten seconds. Then you multiply by six. That will give you the exact number of respirations per minute. Now let me check it before I go." Ken took off his watch and counted imaginary respirations out loud. It came out to twenty per minute. Ken looked at Jordan real seriously and said, "You get the idea, Jordan?"

Jordan nodded and said, "I think I can handle this just fine. You guys go have lunch. I'll stay here." He pulled his watch off and sat down outside the cage in front of the bear and began to count, nodding his head as he followed the imaginary respirations. He got eighteen his first time to check. The culprits did not return for one hour and did not expect to find Jordan there when they got back. They expected that Jordan would eventually realize that the bear wasn't breathing and try to find someone to help. They never counted on him staying there so long.

Jordan smiled at us when we got back and Ken asked, "How's he doing, Jordan?

"He was breathing at about twenty respirations about one minute ago."

"He roll over or anything?"

"No. He's still out like a light."

"Just before you go, Jordan, let's go in and check to see if he's coming out of it."

Ken stepped inside the cage and walked over to the bear. He poked him with his hand, but nothing happened of course. Then he shook him. Then Ken got a real concerned look on his face and bent down and listened for a heartbeat. Ken looked more and more concerned and blurted out, "Jordan, this bear is dead. He's cold, so he must have been dead for a long time. Didn't you see him stop breathing, man?"

Jordan looked panicked. "Man, I didn't see nothin' change from when I got here. I'm sorry he died, but I didn't see him go."

"You stayed right here and counted?"

"Yes sir, I was here the whole time."

"Jordan, this bear's death wasn't your fault. You want to know why?"

"Sure."

"Because he was dead about fifteen minutes before you got here. This was a joke to see how long it would take you to notice you were watching a dead bear."

Jordan got a big friendly smile on his face and said, "Oh, you guys," and laughed as he left the health center. We laughed too. The idea of counting dead bear breaths was funny, and the more we thought about it the funnier it got.

That wasn't the last time that Jordan was caught. We caught him good one lunchtime. Jordan would wolf his lunch down and take a nap every day. We'd have to wake him up or he would sleep for hours. He slept inside the office on top of a long wooden box that was made to hold zoo cleaning agents. It was about seven feet long and fit him fine. He would wad up his jacket into a pillow, and in no time he would be snoring so loud that it was hysterically funny. One day Bob Jenks got the idea that we should black out the windows and door, change the clock to 9:00 P.M., and wait outside until he woke up.

I thought this joke was particularly funny, so I waited with my ear to the door to find out what Jordan would do when he woke up. It was a riot.

When he woke up I heard him moan, "Oh, no! I haven't fed out my animals, and it's 9:20 at night. My wife's going to kill me."

Jordan had a little difficulty getting out the door because of the duct tape from top to bottom. When he burst into the sunlight, it was 12:45 P.M. He smiled and began to laugh. "Oh, you guys," he said as he went to feed his animals, glad to be alive and glad he didn't have to explain why he was three unexplained hours late getting home.

As much as I remember Jordan for these events, he will always be known in my mind as the man who came the closest to being the main course for two very mean Bengal tigers named Henry and Hilda. The incident happened just before the zoo was officially opened to the public as they were putting the finishing touches on the exhibits and filling the cages with animals.

Henry and Hilda had been tranquilized and moved the two miles from the old Griffith Park Zoo to the new Los Angeles Zoo. Jordan Johnson, his supervisor, Bob Wheaton, and the curator of mammals, Ben Haden, were checking the outside portion of their exhibit to make sure there was no broken glass, wire, string, or nails left behind by construction workers or landscape men. It was later discovered that someone had already checked the area and had also authorized the release of the tigers to the outside of the exhibit. The team transporting the tigers arrived ten minutes after Jordan, Bob, and Ben. They even noticed that the door leading to the outside exhibit was open. Though someone checked outside, they didn't see anybody. So they locked the door and prepared to let the vicious Bengals out. The three men outside went unnoticed because they were down in the empty moat finding lots of wire and nails that would create rust spots once the moat was filled with water. They had no idea that soon, very soon, they would be sharing this exploration with Henry and Hilda. I never met the lions that Daniel met in the lions' den, but I can tell you that I would rather take my chances with Daniel's lions any day before being confronted by these Bengals.

As Jordan, Bob, and Ben enjoyed the excitement of being the last men in the exhibit before the tigers were released, a sliding door was being raised only seventy feet away from them. A still slightly dazed Henry ran into the sunlight followed by his mate of several years, Hilda. The men in the moat heard the door slide up, and they knew they should not be hearing that sound. They exchanged panicked looks, each hoping the other could do something. Jordan, being the tallest, stood on his toes to peer above the moat. The expression on his face told the other two men everything they didn't want to know. Jordan was not known to be a religious man, but the others present said he got religion pretty quick, saying something like, "Sweet Lord, help us. We need you now."

They did, too. These two cats were bad news. They hated people.

The three men below had seen the cats, but the cats had not yet noticed them. They crawled on their hands and knees to the wall farthest from the cats and bent down. A crane operator who had been loading boulders into the adjacent exhibits was just returning from his break. He stopped to smoke a cigarette while he took a look at the tigers. As he did so, he thought to himself, *Something is really wrong. There is supposed to be water in that moat. I wonder if anybody knows it's empty.* He bent over to check out the moat and saw the three trapped men huddling next to the wall. He whispered down to them, "I'll drop a hook down and pull you out. Hang in there." He ran to his crane, fired up the engine, and began to swing the cable and hook around to the tiger exhibit. You don't realize just how slow heavy equipment can work until you need something done quickly. The men had their eyes fixed on one location: the top of the opposite wall.

Henry was curious to know the boundaries of his exhibit, so he began to explore. He walked directly to the ledge, where he saw three men looking back at him with stark terror painted all over their faces.

The expressions didn't get better when Henry turned his head, lowered his ears, and roared. He was still a bit groggy and began to walk around the perimeter of the exhibit. Hilda, the meanest of the two, just sat down near the back of the exhibit to let the effects of the drugs wear off. She never saw the men.

The hook and cable descended and hit the ground four feet in front of the terrified men. Ben Haden, the curator, was athletic and leapt for the steel cable. Then he lifted himself hand over hand until he was well out of the reach of any tiger. Bob Wheaton, older and not quite so vital, climbed using his legs until he was out of the tiger's reach.

Jordan was near fainting and had all he could do to run to the cable. He grabbed the cable, jammed his foot in the hook, and, in a higher pitched voice than usual, cried, "Pull this sucker up quick. I feel like tiger bait on the end of this hook. Now pull me outta here before you catch a tiger."

The crane operator gunned the engine and threw the winch into gear. Jordan began to ascend slowly. His eyes were closed and his knuckles pale from gripping the steel cable so tightly. He was finally and mercifully out of harm's way when he was let down to the pavement. They had to pry his fingers loose from the cable and convince him he wasn't in heaven. He survived just fine though he never enjoyed talking about it afterward.

The moat was quickly filled and the crisis averted. However, the guys who caused the communication foul-up got chewed out royally, as you might imagine.

During the summers, scare jokes gave way to water jokes. Nobody was safe from being drenched during the long California summers that sometimes lingered into mid-October. There were several desirable weapons available: water balloons, one-inch high-pressure hoses, buckets, and even fifty-gallon drums. On most hot days someone was getting it good from someone else.

I developed a feud of sorts with my very good friend Bob Pedersen. It was friendly, you understand, but it never ended until the day I left the zoo. During the summers, neither he nor I was safe from the other. One or the other of us constantly felt like he needed to make things even. I always felt it wasn't even unless I got him better than he got me.

One day I obtained an accomplice, Gib Brush, the zoo photographer, and had him request that Bob come out and stand on a particular spot to have his picture taken. Bob was a very compliant person so he came and stood while Gib pretended to focus. Up on the roof seven feet above him, an animal keeper friend and I tipped a hundred-gallon drum forward and dropped all of its contents on Pedersen, nearly knocking him off his feet. The joke almost went too far. Pedersen nearly got angry, but he was left with the consolation that now it was his turn. A few days later I walked around a corner and was nearly knocked off my feet by a huge bucket of water thrown in my face.

I decided to play a very sophisticated joke that would cause him to release the water on himself. I knew that he would be gone for lunch at least forty minutes and began devising my water trap. I filled a surgical glove to capacity with water and was surprised to find that it held nearly a gallon and a half. I carefully laid the filled glove on the chain-link roof just above the door and pulled the canvas tarp back over it. Then I rigged a string and coat hanger together to make a pully that would pop the glove when Pedersen opened the door to clean the outdoor exhibits. I experimented, and it worked every time. It would have been sure to put me one up if it were not for Murphy's law:

If anything can go wrong, it will. I was no sooner through setting my trap when Chester E. Hogan and a delegation of very important people burst through the door heading right for the trap I had just set.

I greeted them and, being the veterinary assistant at the health center, inquired whether there was anything I could do to help them. Mr. Hogan said, "Well, Gary, maybe you could show our friends from City Hall our new cages and tell them a little about the animals that are in them." I was had. I couldn't let them go in first; I had to go first and I did.

I snapped the lock open and pushed open the door. My joke worked perfectly, but the joke was on me. I laughed and said what the famous Jordan Johnson always said, "Oh, those guys." Mr. Hogan didn't know what to do until he saw that the City Hall folks were very amused. Then he smiled and said, "Well, I'm certainly glad that it was you and not us, Gary."

"Yes, sir, I am, too. But it does feel pretty good on this warm day."

Bob Pedersen came back from lunch and saw that I was soaked. Mr. Hogan explained to Bob that someone had gotten me good and that they had all been there to see it. Bob responded that he was very sorry that he hadn't been there to enjoy it himself.

When they left, Pedersen said, "I bet that was meant for me and they showed up and you had to take it rather than let them take it. Right?"

"Right," I answered sarcastically.

"It's sort of like I got you twice before you got me once. That's funny." Then Bob laughed until he was out of breath.

It was funny. And having someone to play with at thirty years of age was a gift.

I thank God for my time at the zoo, both the good and the bad times. I thank God for the rich memories that

I have taken with me to treasure for the rest of my life. I thank God for the friends I made there, especially Dale Thompson, Jack Badal, Edgar Barnett, and Bob Pedersen. I thank God for the wonder, the excitement, the learning, and the growing up that took place during those seven years. I am most thankful that God has been able to use these experiences to touch lives and to glorify Himself.

Barnaby grew to the size of this regal male during the months after his escape. He learned how to survive in the wilderness adjacent to the zoo (see page 181).

The Gelada Named Barnaby

Baboons are really wonderful animals. They are very large and formidable monkeys. They will climb trees but live most of their lives on the ground. There are eight species of baboons, each one bold and stunning in its own way. They are very family oriented, living in troops of twelve to fifty animals. They walk together like an army, with one general and a couple of sergeants in the middle of the troop. The mothers with very young babies accompany them in the center. On the perimeters are the young males, and just one step toward the center the adult females without young.

The general stays at the center because it is equidistant to whatever danger might appear. Should a leopard or hyena or even another troop of baboons arrive, he is off in a flash to defend his troop. They can be savage, but left undisturbed, they are gentle, orderly animals.

Our zoo at one time or another exhibited five of the eight species. This story is about one of the most impressive of the species, the Gelada. The Gelada baboon comes from Ethiopia and lives above 1800 feet in foothills of mountains. They eat fruits, vegetables, and animals, when they can catch them. They are a luxurious dark brown, and the males have the most spectacular long coats of any of the species. Their coat could even be referred to as a mane.

We had nine Geladas in the collection until Barnaby, a teenage male darted past a keeper who was not careful when leaving Barnaby's cage. As social as baboons are, no one believed that this was any big deal. Everyone knew that Barnaby would hang around, and when he got hungry, he could be trapped. A few grapes in a live trap, and, bingo, Barnaby would be home again and back with his family. Everyone but Barnaby knew this.

Barnaby was different. You see, there are always exceptions. Just about the time you think you have an animal figured out, boom, you're in for a surprise.

Barnaby, by human years, would have been about thirteen. He was not half grown but full of spunk and very independent. He was also very intelligent. When the trap was set up near his cage, he would not go near it. He knew what it was and steered clear despite the fact that he was hungry and wanted to eat what was in the trap. His cage was not far from the back fence, and in the early morning hours he began to leave the zoo to go exploring.

The zoo is built in Griffith Park, and Griffith Park adjoins the Hollywood Hills. The zoo is in the midst of thousands of acres of wilderness full of wild animals and patroled by park rangers. The kicker is that this postage stamp of wilderness is surrounded by one of the world's largest cities. This wilderness is made up of the typical brush that covers the foothills in southern California, and the shady canyon areas are made up of oak woodlands. Oddly enough, the area was ideal for Barnaby and not unlike his native habitat in Ethiopia.

Barnaby began to lose a little weight. Those who would see him visit his family made note that his ribs were showing, and some of us were afraid that he might die of malnutrition. But food was our only bait, so he was not fed outside the cage.

His journeys from the zoo became lengthened as hunger drove him into a survival mode. On one of his journeys, he found a spring. Near the spring he found blackberries. Barnaby made a feast, and, for the first time in a long time, he was full when he slept that night.

Days turned into weeks, and the keepers noted that they were seeing Barnaby less frequently. His journeys for food were taking him farther and farther from the zoo, and he was finding a wider range of things he could eat. When he could catch them, he ate locusts and grasshoppers. He also ate lizards. He was trying a variety of leaves and seeds and discovering weekly that there was food everywhere. The weight loss stopped. Barnaby was breaking even until he made a terrific discovery.

One day the brush ended abruptly, and green lawns were everywhere. So were people, so he stayed at the edge of the picnic grounds for fear of being caught.

One morning about 11:30, Barnaby went to visit the picnic area. He came out of the brush face to face with a five-year-old boy eating a peanut butter and jelly sandwich. The boy was fascinated by Barnaby and laughed at him. When the little boy laughed, he showed Barnaby his teeth and opened his mouth. In baboon, this is a challenge to fight, and Barnaby felt discomfort. He was not yet old enough that he would attack, but he knew what it meant. The little boy also stared at him, which was not considered to be polite among baboons. Then this boy did the strangest thing. He threw his sandwich to Barnaby and made sounds that sounded soothing. He was saying "Nice monkey," but to Barnaby, it was just soothing, no more. Barnaby picked up the sandwich and smelled it. It smelled good. He licked it, and it tasted good, so he took a bite. This was a turning point in Barnaby's existence. This is when he crossed the line from survival to abundance. Barnaby discovered that everybody wanted to feed him. He was so full on some days that he turned down food. He was now approaching people and taking the food from their hands. He was still young, so no one was threatened by his appearance. But he was passing through adolescence quickly. He was approaching forty pounds and could eventually weigh a hundred pounds. Barnaby, by nature, was very gentle, unlike his very militant father Ho Chi Minh. There were never any incidents in which people were threatened.

One evening when Barnaby had entertained the picnickers until he was stuffed, he had a very close call. He was on his way back to the zoo where he would visit his mother and extended family and probably sleep. Unknowingly, he passed under a tree where a female mountain lion was surveying the area for something to eat. She had had two bad days of hunting and was both cranky and very hungry. When the predator saw Barnaby she was startled. Her instincts and experience did not prepare her for attacking a baboon outright so she did not leap. She decided to follow Barnaby, now feeling that he looked enough like prey to consider the possibilities. Full grown, Barnaby would be more than a match for an adult female mountain lion, but at fifty pounds he was in trouble.

Barnaby felt uneasy. He didn't know why, but something was wrong. He wasn't hearing enough bird song. The other animals were bothered, and he knew it. The female lioness was downwind, so Barnaby didn't catch her scent. Stealth was her middle name, so he didn't hear her either. Still he knew something was up so he picked up his pace. She picked up her pace also and began to close in on the resourceful young baboon. She snapped a twig and Barnaby heard it. Adrenaline surged through his system as he took flight. The mountain lion heard Barnaby run, and she made an all-out effort to catch him. Barnaby looked back and saw her closing the gap. He leapt into an oak tree and began to climb. His heart began to pound harder when he discovered that she too could climb and nearly as well as he. He was thirty feet up into the branches and realized that she was still closing in. When she was within five feet, he threw himself to lower branches and fell to the ground. She leapt too, but, thinking better of a blind fall through the branches to the ground, she grabbed a branch and hung for a second until she was able to pull herself back into the tree.

Barnaby wasted no time. He ran straight to the zoo fence, which he climbed faster than he had ever done before. It was a close call, and he hoped he would never see her again. He slept fitfully that night and dreamed he was being chased by the female lioness. He leaned against the wire, holding his mother's arm while he slept.

Barnaby was beginning to miss being with his kind. His existence was lonely. Weeks had turned into months, and he was becoming an adult male. He was now seventy-five pounds. Barnaby had a very strong desire to mate that came with his age. But look though he might, there were no baboons in the park. There were nights when he would reach through the chain-link fencing to groom his mother. He felt very attached to her, and her touch was reassuring.

When Barnaby reached ninety pounds and his mane became luxurious, the picnickers began to realize that their children could be at risk. They began to report him to the park rangers, who in turn called the zoo and asked them to step up efforts to recapture the baboon that had been out over a year now.

Meetings were held, and it was decided that Dr. Wordsworth would set up a blind and hide there with a duck hunter. They would simply wait until Barnaby came down to be with his family and dart him with the tranquilizer gun. Barnaby had established a very predictable schedule. He usually came into the zoo about 7:00 P.M. during daylight savings time. It was decided that security should watch for Barnaby's entry into the zoo and see just how predictable he was. It was as if he had a Rolex. He walked across the road that led to his family every night between 7:02 and 7:04.

Barnaby's last week of freedom prepared him for recapture. On Sunday night of that week, Barnaby was taking a long drink at the spring when the female lioness showed up again. Barnaby was afraid but not as afraid as he had been at their last meeting. She didn't look as large to him as she had looked before, and of course he had gained sixty pounds. His canines had grown a full inch and were longer than hers. They stared at each other for several seconds, each waiting to see what the other would do. She growled in a threatening way, and Barnaby's hair stood on end, not because he was afraid but because he wished to threaten back. He pulled back his lips exposing his canines. Then he lurched forward and barked as baboons do when they want to appear aggressive.

The predator knew she was no longer a match for the now-adult male baboon, so she hissed and gave ground. When she had backed up about five feet, she walked away just turning once to hiss. Barnaby never saw her again.

The next Tuesday Barnaby ran into a mated pair of coyotes that had just killed a brush-tailed rabbit. Barnaby loved fresh rabbit so he advanced. He barked and threatened, but the coyotes would not back away from their prey. Barnaby charged, but they both crouched and held their ground. If there had been one coyote, he would have simply attacked and taken the rabbit, but there were two. It was a standoff until a long-submerged instinct surfaced. Barnaby picked up a large rock and threw it at the coyote nearest to him. It hit her in the muzzle, and she yelped. Barnaby found another rock and hit her again. She backed up, but the male stood firm over the rabbit. Barnaby found a large branch with dead leaves and ran at the male, swinging the branch back and forth and making a lot of noise as the branch hit nearby bushes. That did it for Mr. and Mrs. Coyote. They ran and didn't look back.

Barnaby picked up the rabbit and enjoyed it immensely. He peeled it as one would peel an orange. Then he savored his meal.

On Wednesday of that same week, Barnaby reached into a bush to pick up a seed pod and was nearly bitten by a rattlesnake. It frightened him quite badly, and he was jumpy and irritable for the rest of the day.

During the morning he grew a bit impatient when a woman in the park kept withdrawing her offer to give him a piece of apple, so he barked at her and simply yanked it away from her. He had no intention of biting her; he just wasn't in the mood for games. But when the lady represented the incident to the park ranger, she made it sound as though Barnaby was being aggressive and threatening.

The ranger let the zoo know in no uncertain terms that they had better capture Barnaby soon or plan a funeral for him. The zoo assured the ranger that a plan was in effect and Barnaby would be home soon.

Friday evening Dr. Wordsworth carefully prepared a capture dart and loaded it in the rifle. He leaned the rifle against a wall. Then he placed grapes and bananas in a pile in the middle of the road, about forty feet from the blind where he would be hiding when he attempted his shot.

Dr. Wordsworth entered the blind at 6:30 P.M. anticipating Barnaby's arrival. It was daylight savings time, and there was plenty of light and would be until about 8:00 P.M. He stuck the barrel through the viewing slot and kept it aimed near the bananas and grapes.

The evening was beautiful, and Dr. Wordsworth was feeling like the proverbial great white hunter. He was in a lot of shrubbery, and the zoo was full of animals making territorial sounds. The gibbons were hooting, the macaws were screeching, and the lions were providing the bass line to the wild symphony of sounds that filled the valley in which the zoo was nestled.

As it neared 7:00 P.M. the doctor tensed and waited anxiously for Barnaby to show. He was not disappointed. At

7:02 P.M. Barnaby's inner biological clock prompted him to return to the zoo.

He walked up to the grapes and bananas a little suspiciously. They had never been there before, and he wondered why now. He looked carefully in every direction but saw nothing at all out of the ordinary. He walked around the food and bent over to smell it. As he did so, his hindquarters moved into the doctor's gun sight.

The blast of the rifle startled Barnaby, and he ran for the back fence. In seconds he was aware of a sharp stinging sensation and stopped to pull the dart out of his leg. He cleared the first fence, crossed a walking path, and threw himself into the bison yard. His heart was pounding, moving the tranquilizer through his system at a rapid pace. By the time he cleared the bison exhibit, he had just the perimeter fence to jump. He would then be in the wild and free.

He started feeling foggy. The world began turning about him. He reached for the fence, but he couldn't remember why. So he sat down next to it as he watched everything grow dim and roll about like a storm-tossed sea. He saw several animal keepers rushing to him, but he was not afraid, for the drug had taken effect. Nothing really mattered at all; everything went black.

When Barnaby woke up, he was in a fairly large cage at the health center. He had been given a thorough physical examination. Pending any negative results of blood tests, throat cultures, and investigation for internal parasites, he would be reunited with his family after eighteen months in the wild.

The tests only confirmed what we could already see. Barnaby was one of the finest specimens of adult male Gelada baboons in captivity. He was reunited with his family, and his loneliness was cured. Although Barnaby had been very mellow in the wild, he became very dominant in captivity. He displaced his father and became the father of dozens of babies himself. He stayed at the top for several years but has now been replaced by a male that weighs forty pounds more than Barnaby ever did in his prime.

Barnaby's story is wonderful because it so illustrates God's provision for His creatures. The means to survive were always there, but it took Barnaby a while to discover it. He was lean until he began to avail himself of all there was to offer. Barnaby found that there was more than enough to survive. It wasn't a question of survival really but of how abundantly he wanted to live.

One of the Lord Jesus Christ's purposes for coming is expressed in the Gospel of John. "But I came to give life—life in all its fullness" (John 10:10).

> "So I tell you, don't worry about the food you need to live. And don't worry about the clothes you need for your body. Life is more important than food. And the body is more important than clothes. Look at the birds in the air. They don't plant or harvest or store food in barns. But your heavenly Father feeds the birds. And you know that you are worth much more than the birds. You cannot add any time to your life by worrying about it.
>
> "And why do you worry about clothes? Look at the flowers in the field. See how they grow. They don't work or make clothes for themselves. But I tell you that even Solomon with his riches was not dressed as beautifully as one of these flowers. God clothes the grass in the field like that. The grass is living today, but tomorrow it is thrown into the fire to be burned. So you can be even more sure that God will clothe you. Don't have so little faith! Don't worry and say, 'What will we eat?' or 'What will we drink?' or 'What will we wear?' All the people who don't know God keep trying to get these things. And your Father in heaven knows that you need them. The thing you should want most is God's kingdom and doing what God wants. Then all these other things you need will be given to you. So don't worry about tomorrow. Each day has enough trouble of its own. Tomorrow will have its own worries."
>
> Matt. 6:25–34

The Rattlesnake

There are few American animals that have captured our imagination more than the rattlesnake. There could not be more than a handful of Westerns that did not have a scene where someone was bitten by one. My personal favorite was *True Grit* with John Wayne and Kim Darby. Kim Darby falls into a den of rattlesnakes and is badly bitten by a particularly large and ugly specimen. John Wayne pulls out all the stops to get her to a doctor who saves her life. It's a wonderfully adventurous scene and evokes all the fear and mystery that go with the creature that inspires it.

From my earliest days I have been fascinated with rattlesnakes. My grandparents owned a home in Twentynine Palms, California, a typical desert town in the granddaddy of American deserts, the Mojave. Several species of rattlers live in that desert, and my first experience with one occurred when my father was helping my grandparents build their cabin. I was nine at the time. Dad was putting the exterior stucco on the outside of their desert cabin when all of a sudden I heard him scream and throw himself backwards away from the wall he was plastering. He crawled backwards a few steps and stood up, keeping his eyes focused at the ground where last he had plastered. He was pale and shaking violently.

I looked where he was looking but couldn't see a thing. My grandfather came running and asked, "What's wrong, Walt?"

"Rattler!"

"He get you?"

"Darn near."

My father wiped the perspiration from his forehead and went to get a shovel. When he returned, he pulled the small rattlesnake out of the shade and into the hot sun. It crawled sideways.

"Sidewinder," exclaimed my father.

"Small but deadly," mused my grandfather.

The sidewinder is also called the horned rattlesnake because of scaly projections above each eye. Its sandy tan color had blended so well with its surroundings that my father had not seen it, though he had been working right within its striking distance for the last three minutes. It had chosen to hide instead of strike, thank the Lord, and we were all grateful.

My father cut its head off with a shovel. My grandfather skinned it and gave both the rattles, there were five, and the skin to me. I took it to class the following Monday morning and shared my father's close call. All the boys considered me the luckiest boy in the class for having been a part of such an exciting weekend.

Years passed before I was to have such an excellent adventure again. I was eighteen, in fact, when it happened. Right out of high school, I was hired by Campus Life, then called Youth for Christ, as a truck driver/ maintenance man/counselor for their six-day camps. Once again I was in the Mojave Desert, in Hesperia, California. In fact, it was there, at a camp for delinquent and underprivileged girls that I met my wife, Carol. She was a counselor. (You didn't think . . . ? No! She was a cute little number from the beach cities. A real sweet little California Baptist girl.)

It was also there that I met Sonny Salsbury, my lifelong friend and often partner in near or borderline crime. Sonny was twenty-five at the time and my role model. Sonny was a make-things-happen person and always ready to create fun and adventure. We seemed to have everything in common, especially a love for nature. Sonny thought that it would be fun to have a Teen Ranch Zoo, so he constructed several cages and aquariums that we spent every spare minute trying to fill. Desert animals typically come out during the night, so that's when we did most of our bring-them-back-alive activities. We caught several species of snakes and rodents. Kangaroo rats were the most entertaining to catch. This we did by cruising around on the hood of Sonny's Chevelle convertible on desert roads under the unbelievable canopy of stars that shine like diamonds in the Mojave nights. When we saw the kangaroo rats jumping here and there in the sand, we would leap from the hood and chase them with flashlights. We would run around like fools, laughing ourselves out of breath until either they or we gave up.

The one catch that we most wanted eluded us from week to week. We had caught every species of snake known to live in that part of the desert except for some type of rattlesnake. As the weeks passed, we spent more and more time looking, but to no avail. Although we had put together a very impressive little collection, the hallmark of the Old West, the capper, the prize was not a part of it, and we felt like failures.

June gave way to July, which melted into August, and August began to chase September. Still no snake. But we never gave up looking.

Teen Ranch was located in two places ten miles apart. The program and eating took place at a recreation center in Hesperia, but the teens slept in authentic covered wagons located in a canyon. The canyon rested at the base of the north side of the San Bernardino Mountains. Lake Arrowhead is not far, as the crow flies. There were sixteen covered wagons, each of which slept four campers, that circled haybales around a wonderful and rustic campfire. It was very primitive. There was no running water. Two redwood outhouses, which we called the redheads, a canvas water bag, and a windowless storage shed were all that stood on the site. There were no city lights visible, so you really had the feeling that you were in a real wagon train on its way to the gold fields.

Even though we had not seen one rattlesnake the whole summer, we still used their possible presence as a deterrent for teenage midnight exploration. When we held orientation, we had the standard rattler speech.

"Gang, listen up. Many of you will get the urge to explore this canyon or the other wagons after you think that the counselors have gone to sleep. Don't give in to it. The Mojave green rattlesnake crawls at night until the wee morning hours, and any walking other than to the redheads would be foolish and needlessly dangerous. There is no sufficient antivenin should you be bitten, so please be careful, even if you are just walking to the outhouses."

I loved watching the kids when this speech was given. They had big eyes and wiggled nervously on the bales of hay. "Don't go anywhere without your flashlight shining on the ground just a few feet ahead of you. Of course, you can break these rules, but the price of breaking them might be considerably higher and more painful than you can now imagine. We're giving you adult information. We are counting on you to respond to it as adults. Okay, no more about that."

Now Sonny and I are incurable practical jokers. Until

recent years there were some who felt that my practical joking was not only incurable but terminal; that is, they thought that someday someone would kill me to get even. But, alas, I have mellowed. Though I am still up for a good practical joke, it now has to be practical. It was at Teen Ranch that I reached the outer limits of practical joking. Scare jokes are a particular specialty. I had learned how to make a sound with my mouth that was very much like the buzzing of a rattlesnake and decided to use it in a sting operation. One August night after our rattlesnake orientation, Sonny and I waited together until the high-schoolers had begun to drop off to sleep. I got a dinner fork and bent the two middle tines down until they were firmly touching the handle. This of course left the outside tines still in place and about three-quarters of an inch apart. I crawled under a covered wagon and pulled myself quietly next to the exit ladder. When I was in place, Sonny would climb the ladder and call for one of the occupants to come out, saying, "I have something important I need to talk to you about." Now when one of the camp directors says something like that, you get preoccupied, a little worried, deep in thought. You pull on your decent clothing and, half awake, begin to climb down the ladder.

That's when I would make the rattlesnake sound and jab the victim in the leg with the fork. It was a very consistent response that we were able to inspire in the high-schoolers: stark terror. You could hear the screams echoing off of the canyon walls for miles. Then the victims would yell, "I've been bit! I've been bit! I've been bit!" That's when I would yell, "You been had! You been had! It's me. You're going to be fine. You've been bit by a fork. You're going to live."

Then Sonny and I would move to a wagon across the circle and get someone else, after laughing maniacally at our first effort. Now remember, I was eighteen at the time and had not grown up. Sonny had no such excuse, being twenty-five, a husband, and a father.

With two weeks of camp to go, Sonny and I became convinced that we were just not going to see a rattlesnake. Boy, were we wrong. Sonny was going to get one of the closest viewings of a rattlesnake enjoyed by any human in history.

It was Thursday night about eleven o'clock. There was no moon, and the campfire had died down to embers. This was the night that Sonny told "The Legend of the Forbidden Lake," a wonderfully scary story in which, at just the right moment, the staff members reach out to grab several campers and yell "Raaaaaaa" at the top of their lungs. The story had gone very well, and the kids were still buzzing with laughter and excitement over Sonny's expert story telling. Sonny's sister Linda, who happened to be at the camp that week, came running up to him out of breath and said, "Sonny, there's a big rattlesnake under your car! Come quick."

Sonny thought she was joking but followed her to his car, where she said she had seen it crawling under a wheel. She pointed under the car and said, "Sonny, it's there." When she put her hands to her face in fear, Sonny thought she might be covering a smile. He thought to himself, *When I bend over to look, she's going to grab me and scream.* Sonny, next to the car, bent down on his hands and knees and turned on his flashlight. He was face to face with the largest rattler he had ever seen. It was coiled and ready to strike. It couldn't have been more than eighteen inches away from his face and neck, the worst possible places to be bitten. (Did you ever try to put a tourniquet around a neck? Bad medicine.)

Sonny backed away slowly and stood up. He told his sister to keep a safe eye on the snake, and he ran to find me. "Gary, there is a monster of a diamondback under my car. Linda found it. Come help me catch it." We returned to the convertible, and Sonny crawled over the trunk, into the backseat, and then into the driver's seat. He started the car and backed it up until the rattlesnake was clearly illumined in its headlights. Sonny jumped out of the car and ran to the woodpile, where he picked up a one-by-eight piece of wood about eighteen inches long.

Sonny handed me the board and said, "Here's the plan. You pin down the head, and I'll grab the snake behind the neck."

"How far can a snake strike?" I asked, thinking that might be good to know for my part in the capture.

"I'm not sure, but I think it's about a half to one-third of its body length. I think that's what the books say."

"What if this snake didn't read the books, and he's some sort of Olympic striker or something?"

"We'll have to get him to strike a few times so we can find out."

"What you mean we, white man?" I answered in my best Tonto voice. "Sonny, why don't you show me how to pin a rattler down? Then I'll do it."

He did. After making the snake strike several times, we were able to see that he was in the eighteen-inch to two-foot range. Several of the kids who were watching would flinch every time the huge rattler struck. Finally I took over and was able to pin the head. Sonny made a quick grab of the neck just behind the venom sacks at the back of the jaws. He lifted it up and let it hang. The snake was between five and six feet long with a heavy body. It was showing its anger by writhing and rattling like crazy.

There was nothing to house the snake in at the wagon train, but we had a cage already prepared at the recreation center. Sonny said, "Open the car door for me. My hands are a little busy. We have to drive this puppy back to the recreation center."

I let him in quickly and ran for the driver's side. I started the car, and we sped into the night. This was a truly new experience. About every thirty seconds the snake did everything possible to get out of Sonny's grasp. The rattling seemed even louder when the snake's tail was in my lap.

I was wondering what I would do if Sonny lost his grasp on the deadly serpent. Then I decided I would leave the car no matter the speed.

There was a full moon so I could look over and see clearly that I was riding in a car with a five-and-one-half-foot diamondback rattlesnake held by a maniac. Then I realized I was doing this willingly. I began to doubt my sanity. I thought, *Going six-five miles per hour, we should be at the recreation center in ten minutes. Golly, it seemed longer.*

Sonny turned to me and said, "You better hurry."

There was an urgency in his voice that made the statement an imperative. It concerned me. I asked, "Why should I hurry?"

"My hands are perspiring. I don't know how much longer I can hold him."

"Sonny, maybe it would be good if we just stopped and you could let him go."

"No. Just hurry. We've waited all summer for this baby, and we're not going to lose him that easy."

"Let him loose in this car and I'm outta here."

"Just hurry, man."

We mercifully made it to the recreation center. I jumped out of the car and ran around to let Sonny out. I could see beads of perspiration on his forehead and under his nose.

He looked at me weakly and gasped, "My hands are cramping. I don't know if I can let this fella go before he bites me."

I walked with Sonny to the large cage that we had built for rattlesnakes and pondered his dilemma. "Sonny, keep walking to the cage and hold on for two seconds." I ran to the workshop and grabbed a pair of pliers, then ran back to meet Sonny at the cage. I pulled up the lid and said, "Lower his body into the cage and let it hang." He did so. Then I grabbed the snake's mouth with the pair of pliers and held it shut. "Now let go quick," I shouted. I felt the weight of the snake for a second; then I let the snake and pliers both fall into the cage. We had him. We had the biggest rattlesnake I have ever seen in the wild to date. Sonny was exhausted but obviously proud of his accomplishment. He sat down, stared with satisfaction at the Goliath that we had captured, and sighed, "We did it." It has always been a fond memory but one I have never wanted to duplicate. This event occurred just before the part of my brain that makes decisions was fully formed. In retrospect my only justification for doing what we did was that "it seemed like a good idea at the time."

We milked our moment for all it was worth. No matter where in town we went, we bragged about our find. Lou at the riding stables knew. Jean, the checkout lady at the market, knew. We even told people we didn't know about it. Locals brought their children out to see it so they would know what a rattlesnake looked like.

Flo, the lady at the pet store, wasn't impressed. She deflated us a bit when she pulled out Grover, a four-foot king snake and said, "This king snake is more than a match for your diamondback. He'd kill him and eat him for breakfast."

Sonny and I had named our snake Goliath. Though we had no particular fondness for him at the time, her comments evoked a certain foolish pride and misplaced sense of loyalty that inspired us to make a challenge. We told her, "We bet our snake can beat your snake," and she went for it.

Well, Sonny and I fantasized that we had a possible money-raising scheme in our hot little hands. We thought about charging people admission to see Grover and Goliath battle to the death. A lot of people sounded interested when we told them about it, but only a few made any sign of a commitment to show up for the fight. Well, the money-making was a complete bust, but about fifteen people showed up to see who would win the grudge match.

Every piece of literature we could get our hands on said that these two reptiles were natural enemies and there was sure to be action. Well, let me tell you what happened. Nothing happened. When we put Grover in the aquarium, he crawled over to Goliath, curled up like they were best friends, and went to sleep. We tried stirring them up, but they would not be stirred. People looked at each other, smirked, made wise cracks about wasting their Saturday morning, and then they excused themselves for some real excitement at the supermarket.

We returned Grover with the message that we won because he was too afraid to fight. Flo took her snake proudly, announcing he just wasn't in the mood.

As the days passed, the other youth workers at Teen Ranch made it clear that they were not in the least excited about our keeping a deadly rattlesnake at the camp. They made us promise to kill him or let him go far from the camp. We opted for eating him, having heard that rattlesnake tastes just like chicken and is considered by many to be a delicacy.

The next week we were hosting a camp for East Los Angeles gang members from the number-one problem gang in the United States at the time, The Diamond Street Gang. Sonny thought they would get a kick out of eating diamondback rattlesnake, so we sacrificed him, skinned him, and froze him to be cooked.

The next week was memorable to say the least. Working with a dangerous gang can provide unique adventures, and it did. On the last night of camp, the gang expressed their appreciation for a free fun-filled week by slashing the canvas wagon tops with their switchblades and writing graffiti everywhere. We were threatened and pushed around. Many of our possessions were stolen. That week I knew in my heart that dangerous-gang ministry would not have a place in my future.

In spite of their behavior, we were committed to leading them to Christ. One boy's response to Christ's call made the week's trouble worthwhile. Alex was the vice president, which I think in their way of thinking made him second in charge of vice. He kept his decision to himself for a while, but from what I was told by the team that did inner-city ministries, he did fine later.

We brought out the rattlesnake on Friday night and cooked it over the dying embers of a campfire at the end of coat hangers. It was unseasoned, and everyone overcooked their piece. The consensus was that if we had barbecued jogging shoes and eaten the pieces, we would have improved our evening. Well, at least we could all say that we had eaten rattlesnake, although I have since been asked why I would admit it.

One morning years later my pastor posed a question that indicts me whenever I remember this story. "Man may make his plans, but is God in them?" I'm not sure, but I believe he obtained the thought from Proverbs 19:21: "People can make many different plans. But only the Lord's plan will happen."

So much of what we did was either wrong, unwise, or uncalled for. It was wrong to endanger our lives. More than 90 percent of rattlesnake bites occur when people are needlessly handling them. I discovered later that I am deathly allergic to horse serum. That would have been given to me had I been bitten by a rattler and would have been more dangerous to me than the venom of the snake.

I have since realized that I was a role model that night, and thirty boys were given the impression that catching rattlesnakes by hand was manly and possible. Working at the zoo, I discovered that even the experts rarely handle poisonous snakes. They use catching devices and snake hooks to move them. They all say that if you handle them enough, sooner or later you will be bitten.

We needlessly killed an animal that does not enjoy much sympathy from the public even though, on the day God made it, He said it was good. He said it was good because it fulfills a divinely assigned purpose. Rattlesnakes kill rodents, which enjoy a bit more approval but do more damage and spread disease. Goliath was an old snake and had fulfilled a lot of purpose, but we stopped all that so that we could say we ate rattlesnake.

We were caught up for a moment with a money-making scheme and consumed with the idea of impressing people with our bravado. Bottom line: I was showing off, and I feel a little stupid admitting that to you.

I am still convinced that life needs to have adventure and be relaxing and fun, but never at the expense of my character, someone else's feelings, or some animal's life. I hope that now I think about my motives and whether or not my activities have value. I do not want to become obsessed with a legalistic approach to life, but I do want to think twice before I allow the immaturity that governed my life at eighteen to guide my steps in adulthood.

As I close this chapter I want to share with you a few things about God's amazing invention the rattlesnake. I should say inventions, because there are at least twenty-eight known species of them. I believe my state, California, has more of the total twenty-eight than any other state. Let me name a few: the western diamondback, the red rattlesnake, the southern Pacific rattlesnake, the Mojave green rattlesnake, the Panamint rattlesnake, Willard's rattlesnake, and the speckled rattlesnake.

Bees kill more people every year than do rattlesnakes. In fact bees account for more deaths than all of the other poisonous stings and bites put together. Children under three years and people with very high blood pressure are at greatest risk when bitten by a rattlesnake.

Of the bites that occur, 90 percent occur when people attempt to hold a snake. Of the remaining 10 percent, 9 percent are bitten when they inadvertently step on or place their hand on a rattlesnake. Only 1 percent are bitten by snakes who strike out at them.

Members of the rattlesnake family are endowed with heat-sensing devices in their faces. They can sense a quarter of a degree difference in temperature from four feet away. They have one heat-sensitive nerve on each side of their face. When both are feeling the same temperature, they strike and hit what they feel. We designed our missile guidance systems after these heat-sensing devices.

Rattlesnakes have incredible powers of taste. A rattlesnake licks the air and waves his tongue back and forth. A sticky substance on his tongue picks up molecules, which he drags across the Jacobson's sensing organ in his mouth. His brain interprets the taste. If it is food (rodents), the snake will follow a trail until he tastes so many rodent molecules that his instincts tell him he has come to the rodents' home. Then the snake simply waits for the food to walk by. Whap! It's dinner time.

The rattlesnake grows his whole life, though as he gets older the growth process slows down considerably. There is a myth that the venom of young rattlesnakes is more concentrated than that of the adults. That is not true.

In recent years we have experienced the consequences of one of our sins. You see, we have felt compelled to kill rattlesnakes whenever and wherever we find them. The ones we found were usually found because they rattled in fear, betraying their whereabouts. This practice left behind the rattlers that were least afraid of man to breed with others that were not afraid of man. Now more people step on them because they are less frequently warned of their presence. It is foolish to label evil what God during the Creation declared to be good.

The best advice is to leave rattlesnakes alone when we see them in the wild or move them back to the wild areas when we see them in housing areas that border the wild. That could be accomplished by slipping a rake handle under the middle of the snake's body and lifting it into an empty trash can. Then just take it out and let it go. Sounds crazy but it's sound ecological practice. Trust me.

Should you ever be bitten, the best practice is to get to medical help as soon a possible. Sixty percent of the time snakes give a warning bite and withhold their venom. The rest of the time, you are at a very low risk of dying, so do not panic or do anything to increase your heartbeat. Just walk slowly or be carried to help and stay calm. If you do anything, and most recommend simply getting to a doctor, just place a tourniquet between the site of the bite and your heart; then tighten it for twenty seconds and loosen it for ten. The idea is to meter the blood flow to the heart area slowly but not to stop it altogether. Do not leave the tourniquet on indefinitely unless you would like to lose whatever is bitten. Whatever you do, don't cut. The snake's fangs are curved, so you are not cutting where the venom was actually injected. The cutting leads to bleeding and infections.

These creatures are ugly and attractive, sometimes deadly, unpredictable, covert, possessed of amazing abilities—but also the handiwork of God. I guess you could say the same about humans, and you wouldn't kill them. So please consider not killing the rattlesnake. They are life. Please don't take it.

The Zoo's Worst Night

When I was thirteen I walked across a graveyard at midnight with two of my closest friends. I think it was a rite of manhood, but I was never sure. Doug and Ronny pretended to be brave as did I, but when we told the story later to friends, we all confessed that we had been afraid, not terrified but afraid. I remembered that my heart began to pound halfway across when I realized that we were smack dab in the middle of about ten thousand dead bodies. I wondered if one of them might reach out of the ground and pull me into a casket for a little conversation.

It was a moonless night and, not wanting to be caught by the security guard, we had no flashlight to show us the way. The only illumination came from street lights more than four hundred feet from where we walked. We had picked a still, foggy night in October for our journey into darkness. The mature trees in this old graveyard cast vague shadows and forms that leaned into us as we walked. The only sounds we heard came from distant dogs and our own muffled footsteps. I hated dead people, and this whole dumb idea had come from telling Doug and Ronny about my experiences at my grandfather's funeral.

Sheldon was my step-grandfather but the only grandfather I had ever known on my father's side. He had been the captain of a sport fishing boat, a small but stout-hearted craft named the *Star and Crescent.* I never saw Grandpa Sheldon without a pipe in his mouth. It was a part of him and never seemed to stay lit. He always wore a heavy, dark-blue, Navy-issue coat, whether it was warm or cold, and a faded-black captain's hat that smelled of fish and perspiration. Grandpa taught me how to fish and how to stand at the helm and guide the sturdy little boat to port. It was seaworthy and good in a wind, for one so small. She could only hold thirty-four passengers, but their fare more than paid the bills in the early fifties.

Because I was Grandpa's favorite grandchild, my grandmother chose me to accompany her to the slumber room of the funeral home, where Grandpa lay deader than a mackerel in a fancy casket. She took my hand and led me right up to the casket, having no idea that I had never seen a dead person before. I looked over my shoulder for help from my dad. I begged him with my eyes to rescue me, but he only motioned me forward. His eyes told me to be a comfort to my brokenhearted grandmother. So I turned and stared at my dead grandfather, while my grandmother spoke through tear-filled eyes. "He loved you so, Gary. You were his favorite."

Then without warning she placed my warm hand on his, and the world stopped turning. I stopped breathing and stared at his eyes, waiting for them to open suddenly. The coldness of his hand spread to mine and traveled up my arm until I felt cold and clammy all over. I thought I was going to throw up all over the new suit that they had bought him for the occasion, but I didn't. Somewhere far away I heard my grandmother's voice droning on, "Doesn't he look like he's resting? He needed a rest; he's worked hard all of his life. Now he can rest." He looked dead to me. He looked like he felt. And he felt dead. He looked thin, and they had put a lot of make-up on him. It probably looked fine from about twenty feet away, but up close it made him look dead. My grandmother mercifully removed my hand from his and pressed it against her warm cheek where I could feel her tears. I was glad I hadn't thrown up.

If I live to be one hundred, no human shall ever receive from me a token of love more sincere than I bestowed on my grandmother when I let her lay my hand on the hand of my dead grandfather. It was a noble sacrifice. If anyone could comprehend the courage I exhibited that day in that slumber room, they would be moved to write an epic poem to depict it or paint a masterpiece to capture it. But alas I'm about the only one who will ever really know what I did for Grandma. Some of my friends were pretty impressed anyway.

Doug and Ronny and I finished our graveyard walk at 12:10, and as far as I know we never woke anybody up. We all felt a little braver for the walk but have never had any desire to repeat it.

As exciting as a graveyard is at midnight, it is no match for a large zoo at the same hour. Graveyards are full of imagination, zoos reality. When you hear something growling in the night at a zoo, it came from something real that you hope is still in its cage. Zoo roads twist and turn, winding on and on. Trees and bushes abound to conceal any hidden thing. The Los Angeles Zoo had had so many animals escape in its early days that you never felt really safe at night. I have been through the zoo on many nights for various reasons, and I would choose a graveyard over a night-time zoo for recreation any time.

I wondered how the night security guards kept their sanity while checking the zoo late at night month after month. I am sure one guard didn't fare so well. It was the zoo's worst night when he lost it, and he lost it big.

Hans Gruber said he didn't mind when he pulled night duty. He was for the most part a loner, not by his own choosing, I think, but because there was so much about him to avoid. Hans loved and collected guns. He was forever trying to get someone to listen to him expound on what a big hole a .44 caliber pistol could make in a person or animal. Hans hated everyone, but he said it wasn't prejudice to say the things he did because what he said was fact. Once, trying to demonstrate his openness and liberality, he said he would date Jewish chicks except he didn't want to take a chance that he might fall in love with one. Exasperated, I asked him why not. He floored me when he explained that Jewish chicks age twice as fast as blond-haired German men and he didn't want anybody thinking he had married an old lady when he grew older. I asked him how he knew this to be true. He said it was just his observation after years of watching Jews and "regular people."

Still, I tried to be friendly with Hans because I felt sorry for him. I felt that's what God would have me do. Although there were some pretty good reasons for Hans to feel lonely, I still felt compelled to talk to him when he delivered mail to the health center.

I frightened Hans one day when he was running down the Jews. He had just made a comment about big-nosed Jews when it dawned on him that my nose was large. He said, "By the way, Richmond, you're not Jewish are you?" I just nodded yes and walked away as if I were disgusted. Jesus was in me, and I felt that qualified me in some mysterious way to be a little Jewish anyway. Hans was flustered, but he apologized. I told him that that was okay. I understood that he was raised to think the way he did about Jews, and I was used to people making fun of my nose. It was enlightening to see the way that he reacted to me after that. He wanted to be friends as we had been but wasn't quite sure that he could. I continued to be friendly but could feel the struggle within him when he was in my presence.

I finally decided to tell him that I was not Jewish but would be proud to be if I was. I told him that my Lord was Jewish and that the Jews were God's chosen people. I also asked Hans not to make comments that made Jews sound inferior when he was around me because it hurt my feelings. He didn't after that, and we got along fine.

When Hans drew night duty, I rarely saw him. I sort of missed our inane conversations and kidding.

No one knew that night duty was taking its toll on Hans, and he wouldn't admit it to anyone. Because he was frightened, he had gone against zoo policy and begun carrying a gun in his security vehicle for his own protection. He had been startled by transients and teenagers who had crawled over and under the fences into the zoo. Running into a ragged street person looking for food or a group of older teens crashing the zoo on a lark at 2:00 A.M. could take the wind out of anyone's sails.

In June of 1968 a blanket of fog settled over the Los Angeles Zoo every night. By 9:00 P.M., the visibility was about forty feet, even with foglights. Hans was on his second run, checking seven miles of interior zoo roads. He was more on edge than usual from the strain of driving under these conditions, and his eyes darted back and forth trying not to miss anything unusual. Even though it was cool, he was perspiring. When he finished his run, he reported in at the security office to visit the restroom and splash cool water in his face. He recorded in the log that everything was normal and told Mr. Williams that he was going to inspect the old zoo.

The old zoo was two miles from the main zoo and was being used for a holding compound. Having been built in 1937, it was rustic and all the trees were fully grown. Because the zoo public was not allowed to see it any longer, the landscaping had been allowed to become overgrown. The tight little canyon where the old zoo was located was dark and eerie. Sounds were magnified, giving the illusion that anything you heard was right next to you. You knew as soon as you entered the gate that you were on your own. If you were attacked by man or beast, there would be no help for a long while. Entering was always a little act of bravery.

When Hans entered the old Griffith Park Zoo, he patted his revolver to make sure he had a good sense of its location. He left the vehicle and loosed the chain holding the gate fast. Fog swirled around the headlights of the security vehicle and created a mystical atmosphere. Hans was uneasy. Adrenaline was surging through his veins, and his heart was pounding for no reason that he could discern. He drove his vehicle just inside the gate and got out of the car to replace the chain. He had the eerie feeling that he was being watched, and he was right.

Susie, a petite, six-year-old chimp, stared into the night where the fog was aglow. She heard the whirring of the car engine. It was a familiar sound, one that she heard four times nightly. She shouldn't have been seeing the glow of the headlights, but she had escaped earlier that evening and was out for a walk in the fog-shrouded old zoo. She stared with interest as the headlights drew near. She liked people, and a little company would be fine. None of the other chimps had joined her. She had been thoughtful enough to close the cage door behind her, although she had left the back door to her exhibit open. From where she was standing, she could vaguely see Hans getting out of the car. The light inside the car stayed on, and she walked towards it as Hans walked away from it. When she got to the car, Hans was several yards away checking the locks on the cage doors.

Susie saw the gun on the front seat and was very uncomfortable. All the chimps recognized guns from the guns with painful tranquilizer darts that were used on them each year before their physical exams. She decided that she didn't want to be anywhere near the gun, so she set out to find Hans for a little companionship.

Hans had just discovered the open back door of her exhibit. He entered slowly to see if anything was out of order. Since he didn't remember the number of chimpanzees in the collection, he didn't realize that one was missing. He smiled as he recorded in his notebook that the door had been left open. He didn't like Elvin Rayburn, their keeper, and was glad to report that he had fouled up. He tucked his black steel flashlight under his chin and pulled out his notebook and a pen. While he was making his notes, Susie walked up silently behind him and patted his leg to greet him.

His reaction could not have been more dramatic if it had been a Middle Eastern terrorist. He threw himself against the wall of the exhibit and dropped his flashlight, breaking the bulb. As it fell, he caught a glimpse of Susie running away. He had screamed so loud that she could only believe something dangerous was about. She wasn't going to stay there and face it either. No, sir. She would run and hide until it was safe.

The thought of being that close to an ape catapulted Hans toward the car. He fell twice scrambling through the darkness, guided only by the glow of the headlights and the sound of the engine. He was hyperventilating and nearly fainted as he threw himself into the car and slammed the door. He lay back in the seat waiting for his heart to stop pounding. He didn't want to sound terrified when he called the main zoo to announce the emergency.

"Security Two to Security One, come in please."

"Security Two, go ahead please."

"We have an ape of some sort out over here. What should I do? Over."

"Standby, Security Two, while I find out."

The young security guard at the main zoo looked at the policy manual under escaped animals and saw that there were five numbers to call. He chose Dr. Hart because he was the most approachable. Although he was a world-renowned scholar in his field, Dr. Hart seemed always to have the time and the inclination to be friendly. The vast majority of the zoo staff would have died for him without being asked. He was, and still is, a great man.

Dr. Hart had gone to bed early that night and was asleep when the security guard called. Mrs. Hart answered the phone and had to wake him from a very deep sleep to come to the phone.

"Hart here," the vet said, rubbing his eyes and trying to get a grip on reality.

"Doc, we got an ape loose at the old zoo. What do we do?"

"That would be a chimp. Could be real dangerous if it got out of the zoo into residential Griffith Park. Chimps could do some real damage. They can be very dangerous. Do anything you can to keep it from getting out of the zoo." Dr. Hart was still waking up and more thinking out loud than giving orders. "I'll be there in twenty minutes. Call Ed and Tony and tell them to meet me at the old zoo."

"Sure, Doc, anything you say."

When Dr. Hart began to wake up, he wondered which security guard was working patrol that night. He was hoping that it wasn't Hans because he knew Hans would blow everything out of proportion. Well, he'd be there in twenty minutes and not much could happen in that time. He finished dressing, jumped in his MG, and headed for the zoo at top speed.

"Security Two to Security One, help's on the way. Hart says you got a loose chimp over there and that they can be real dangerous. He says we can't let it get out of the zoo because if it got to the homes, it could do some real damage, maybe hurt someone real good. I don't know what to tell you to do but that's what he said."

Hans put his hand on his revolver and replied, "I'll do everything I can."

He stared into the fog. Holding his revolver gave him a sense of power and confidence. He pulled it out of his holster and held it in his lap for several seconds. He then stepped out of the car and stared into the night, searching the shadows for some evidence of the escaped chimp. He couldn't see her, but she could see him.

Susie watched as Hans looked in all directions. He wasn't screaming anymore, so the danger must have passed. She began cautiously walking toward Hans.

The more Dr. Hart thought about what he had said the more he wished he had not painted such a dangerous picture of the chimps. He wished he had just waited until he got there to take care of it himself. Finally, he made the turn-off to the zoo and sped past the security office to pick up the tranquilizer gun and his black bag.

Meanwhile, Hans saw movement in the lights in front of the car. It was Susie. His heart began to pound. He may as well have had a lion stalking him. Remembering the warning he had been given, he judged that Susie was acting aggressively by approaching him at all. He slowly lifted his revolver and pointed it at her chest.

Susie looked up at Hans. The headlights were blinding her, but she could see that he was pointing something at her. She slowed her approach. When she was about ten feet away, she could see that he was pointing a gun at her. Terrified, she ran into the night as Hans pulled the trigger.

Dr. Hart pulled up to the old zoo gate, quickly threw the gate open, and drove in without bothering to shut the gate behind him. He could see the glowing lights of the security vehicle. Skidding to a halt next to it, he jumped from the car.

Hans greeted him with a satisfied look on his face. "Emergency's over, Dr. Hart. The ape tried to charge me, and I had to shoot it."

"What? Where is it, quick? Take me to it," Dr. Hart begged.

Hans led him just ten feet to where Susie lay face down in the leaves and dirt. The doctor dove for her, lifted her up, and moved her into the lights of the vehicle. She was limp in his arms. He carefully laid her down and pressed his ear to her chest. There was no heartbeat or pulse or reflexes. She was dead, and there would be no bringing her back.

Dr. Hart began to sob. He held Susie in his lap and rocked her back and forth as though she were a child, his child.

Hans, confused, asked, "Did I do wrong?"

Dr. Hart looked up with tear-filled eyes and replied, "Hans, this was Susie. She used to be a pet. She was the tamest chimp in the collection. I set you up to kill the tamest chimp in our collection. This is my fault."

"It looked like she was charging me. I was just protecting myself."

"She was probably trying to make friends, Hans, but you wouldn't have known because I told you guys how dangerous our chimps were. It's not your fault."

The other keepers arrived in time to see Dr. Hart gently lay the chimp in his car so that he might take her to the main zoo. He was teary, and no one spoke because they didn't know what to say. Dr. Hart stayed several hours that night because he decided to perform her necropsy to determine exactly why she had died. What he discovered bothered him a great deal, but he didn't know what to do with the information. The chimp had not been shot in the chest as Hans had claimed but in the back. She must have thought Hans was holding a tranquilizing gun, and she was running away from it when he shot. Hans had not wanted her to get out of the zoo. Dr. Hart felt worse than ever. He knew that somehow his directions had inspired this moment, and he knew that no one would want to believe it. They would want to believe that Hans was a gun-happy jerk and blame the whole mess on him.

That's exactly what happened. The harder Dr. Hart tried to accept the blame for what had happened the more the zoo personnel sought to exonerate him and blame Hans. They would say,"Isn't it just like Hart to take the blame for someone? Well, we know that gun-happy Kraut was the real criminal." No matter where Hans went after that, keepers would turn their backs to him or pretend to shoot him with their fingers. They called him names like Chimp-killer.

Hans would try to smile, but it was plain that he felt more alone than ever. He spent more time at the health center because we were kind to him. His visits were temporary sanctuary from the cruel storm that assailed him when he drove through the rest of the zoo.

The keepers never really let go of the event. After they added Susie's death to Hans's prejudice and isolationist policies, they made him a social outcast, an untouchable.

I was frustrated by the situation. Hans needed to be loved as much as any man I have ever known, but a disastrous moment now made that an unlikely possibility. I didn't like what he had done, but when I put myself in his position I could not say for sure that I would not have done the same thing.

1. He had been working under very stressful conditions at night. The zoo is a frightening place at night.
2. Hans didn't know one chimp from another. It wasn't his job. Some of the chimps, especially Jeanie and Toto, would have been unpredictably dangerous.
3. The information by which Hans made his decisions had been given by a very reliable man, a world authority. He had said chimps were very dangerous and ought not to be allowed to leave the zoo.
4. The zoo didn't allow their security force to carry guns, but Hans had a license and as a private citizen was within his rights. (After that incident a written policy was issued forbidding the security force from being armed.)

It was too late for Susie, but no animal has been killed since that time.

5. The security guards were never trained to handle any animal emergency.

This incident truly represented the zoo's worst night. Nothing so unjust or frustrating has occurred since, at least at the zoo.

I hate to think about this incident. To relive it frustrates me. It does illustrate the reality of this present age, some of what is and has been true since the fall. Life is full of confusion. Life isn't fair. Misunderstanding abounds, and death is all around us. These were the consequences when Adam and Eve chose to be the god of their own lives.

I don't like this story, but not a week of my life goes by without the nightly news revealing one ten times worse. Headline: "Drive-by Shooting Takes Life of Innocent Six-Year-Old." As unjust as this night's events were, they don't begin to match the injustice that occurs every day in every country in the world. Injustice, confusion, and futility are par for the course in a fallen world, a world ruled by the prince of darkness.

Thanks be to God that the time will come when "we will all be changed. It will only take a second. We will be changed as quickly as an eye blinks. This will happen when the last trumpet sounds. The trumpet will sound and those who have died will be raised to live forever. And we will all be changed" (1 Cor. 15:51b–52).

We are going to be made perfect and so will our circumstances. There will be no more tears, no more injustice or confusion, only joy at God's right hand forevermore. Sound too good to be true? You can believe it .

But until that day, we are living in enemy-occupied territory. Injustice and unfairness are going to be the rule, not the exception. The truth is that if you are not currently singing a song of sadness, you will be. It has many verses, and you ought to know them so that when you are given your chance to sing you might sing well. Job sang all the verses. He best illustrates what it means to be a victim of injustice. He knew sadness to a degree that you and I will never know, but he still praised God with his life.

Several dictionaries I consulted offered the following definitions of sadness: the feeling of being low in spirit; having the blues; the absence of joy; feeling down, disheartened, dejected, disappointed, depressed, depleted, disconsolate, and downcast (I put all the D words together myself). Sadness also includes the feeling of being forsaken, lonely, abandoned, and in the pits.

Sadness comes in mild forms, like when you wanted crispy at Colonel Sanders' but all they had was regular. Sometimes sadness comes in industrial strength, like when you lose your mate to death or divorce or you experience the loss of a child.

Sometimes all it takes to treat sadness is a word of encouragement. Then again there are times when you are beyond consolation for a long time, as was Rachel when she lost her beloved Joseph.

Let's look at the world authority on sadness, Job. His story is told in the Book of Job, found just before the Book of Psalms in the Old Testament. Job experienced every form that sadness takes. Let's review what he went through in just the first three chapters of his book.

1. Job lost his means of making a living as a rancher and farmer. When Satan unleashed his cold, calculated attack to discourage Job, he took the oxen, the cattle, and the servants who did the plowing. Then the fire of God fell and killed the sheep and the servants that cared for them. The camels, which would have been used to take his crops to market, were also stolen. Bottom line: Job was wiped out. He was broke, with no economic base on which to rebuild, and he was

too old he thought to start over. A man's identity is in his profession, and Job was stripped.

2. Job lost his children, seven sons and three daughters, all in the same day. He was a terrific father. We know this because he prayed for his children every day. He cared deeply for them and their walk with God. Can you even imagine how he must have felt losing ten children on the same day?
3. Job had a terrible marriage, one in which his wife was an aggressive discouragement to him. When Satan was allowed to do anything he wanted to do to Job, he took his children but not his wife. That's why we know he had a lousy marriage. Job's wife encouraged him to curse God and die.
4. Job lost his health. He was covered with infected boils from head to toe. There was no comfortable way to lie or sit. The infection was not only painful but made him smell foul.
5. Job was disfigured by his disease; his friends wept when they saw him. People turned away and ridiculed him for his grotesque appearance.
6. Job's friends all turned their backs on him, so he was very lonely at the time when he most needed support.
7. Job hadn't done anything to deserve these calamities, which made it very difficult to comprehend why they were happening.
8. Job no longer felt God's favor and did not sense His presence. Job's closest friend seemed to be turning His back.

9. Job's friends began to assume he was being punished for some hidden sin. They verbally abused him for the better part of a year.
10. Satan himself was the agent of Job's oppression, and Satan is the most powerful evil being in the universe. The heaviness of Job's spirit must have been awesome.

I have thought about it, and I can't think of anything to add to the trial that would have made it worse. His pain must have been indescribable. Through it all Job did not curse God, for he knew and had accepted that it was God's right to allow these things in his life.

The Book of Job proves that bad things happen to good people and that they should not be viewed always as punishments but as tests. The word for *trials* and *tests* is the same in the New Testament. These events in our lives have one of two effects. They either make us bitter or better.

We should ask the Lord if we are being punished for something as did Job. If we can see that we are not, then we are left with the knowledge that our character is being developed. Asking why is permitted, but asking for help is better because "Why me?" never brings a solution to our dilemma.

There is bad news and good news. First the bad because I want to end on a good note. Everyone who reads this will experience some of the things on Job's list periodically in their lives. Some more, some less. But if we live long enough, we will most likely experience most of the things on the list. That's the bad news.

The good news has two parts. The first part is that these sorrows don't go on forever. They have an end. God wants us to know this, because He has given us so many Scriptures that convey this thought. If you are now going through some industrial-strength sadness, read the following Scriptures. They should encourage you.

> Their gladness and joy will fill them completely. Sorrow and sadness will go far away (Isa. 35:10).
>
> Your sun will never set again. Your moon will never be dark again. This is because the Lord will be your light forever. And your time of sadness will end (Isa. 60:20).
>
> They will be like a garden that has plenty of water. And the people of Israel will not be troubled anymore (Jer. 31:12).
>
> I will give them comfort and joy instead of sadness (Jer. 31:13).
>
> Although the Lord brings sorrow, he also has mercy. His love is great (Lam. 3:32).
>
> I tell you the truth. You will cry and be sad, but the world will be happy. You will be sad, but your sadness will become joy (John 16:20).
>
> Now you are sad. But I will see you again and you will be happy. And no one will take away your joy (John 16:22).

You must read Job 42:12–16. You will discover that trials do not last forever. Job was vindicated and blessed beyond his wildest imagination. God is just.

The second part of my good news is that we benefit from experiences that produce intense sadness. God knows how much we can take and what we need to develop our character. Part of being His child means trusting God to bring into our lives only that which is necessary to achieve His purposes. Consider the following Scriptures, and see if they help you to yield to His sovereign hand or accept the trial you are now facing.

"Because of disaster, troubles and sadness, their families grew smaller and weaker" (Ps. 107:39). Sorrow is a highly prized character trait that comes with sadness. In Isaiah 66 God makes it clear that He shows favor to the humble.

"With much wisdom comes much disappointment. The person who gains more knowledge also gains more sorrow" (Eccles. 1:18). Deep learning comes through sorrow, and wisdom accompanies it. They say that ignorance is bliss, but I know of no one who would remain ignorant. The wisest people I know have suffered greatly. There is no other path to greatness.

"Sorrow is better than laughter. Sadness has a good influence on you" (Eccles. 7:3).

"He was hated and rejected by people. He had much pain and suffering. People would not even look at him. He was hated, and we didn't even notice him" (Isa. 53:3). Isaiah is telling us we are like Christ when we are sorrowful.

The apostle Paul said, "Now I am happy, but not because you were made sad. I am happy because your sorrow made you change your hearts" (2 Cor. 7:9). Sometimes it takes a prolongedly saddened heart to lead us to ask God's forgiveness. Sadness must be considered a good thing if it can bring us back to God.

In 2 Corinthians 7:11, Paul presents a shopping list of the benefits of sorrow. He tells us that sadness produces godly sorrow, a desire to be good; it makes us appalled by sin; it makes us concerned about sinning; it brings a desire for God; it gives us a concern for others and a love for justice.

Closing thought: God intends to heal our grief and sorrow.

"Lord, surely you see these cruel and evil things. Look at them and do something. People in trouble look to you for help. You are the one who helps the orphans" (Ps. 10:14).

David gives us a good example of what we need to do to relieve sorrow. "Lord, have mercy. I am in misery. My eyes are weak from so much crying. My whole being is tired from grief" (Ps. 31:9).